Living in Step

Living in Step

RUTH ROOSEVELT

JEANNETTE LOFAS

McGRAW-HILL BOOK COMPANY
New York St. Louis San Francisco Bogotá Düsseldorf
Madrid Mexico Montreal Panama Paris São Paulo
Tokyo Toronto

First McGraw-Hill Paperback Edition, 1977
345678910 MUMU 89876543210
Reprinted by arrangement with Stein and Day, Publishers

Library of Congress Cataloging in Publication Data

Roosevelt, Ruth.
Living in step.

Reprint of the ed. published by Stein & Day, New York.
Bibliography: p.
1. Family. 2. Stepchildren. 3. Stepmothers. 4. Stepfathers. I. Lofas, Jeannette, joint author. II. Title.
[HQ734.R75 1977] 301.427 77-7235
ISBN 0-07-053596-5

To our families
and all families
living in step

•/•

Contents

•/•

Acknowledgments

FIRST WE'D LIKE to thank Patricia Day, our publisher and editor, who also lives in step, whose intelligence and foresight have made *Living in Step* possible. We'd also like to thank all the many stepfamilies and steppersons who have openly related their step experiences to us. To the experts who took time to share their insights, we'd like to extend our special appreciation:

L. Dean Baxter, M.D., Child Psychiatrist, County Mental Health, Denver, Colo.

Jean Criner, M.A., Dir. of Therapeutic Educational Center, San Francisco, Calif.

Esther Oshiver Fisher, Ph.D., Marital Counselor, New York City.

Richard A. Gardner, M. D., Child Psychiatrist and Psychoanalist, member of the faculties of Columbia University and William Alanson White Psychoanalytic Institute, New York City.

Shepard D. Gellert, Redicision Institute for Transactional Analysis, Huntington, New York.

Sidney Gerhardt, M.S.W., Psychiatric Social Worker, Stamford, Conn.

Anne H. James, M.S.W., Program Supervisor, Family and Children's Aid, Norwalk, Conn.

Quinton C. James, M.D., Child Psychiatrist, Los Angeles, Calif.

Herma Hill Kay, Ll.B., Prof. of Law, University of California, Bolt Hall, Berkeley, Calif.

L. Warde Laidman, M.S.W., Clinical Assistant, Community Mental Health Service, San Francisco, Calif.

John Leanard, M.D., Psychiatrist, Chairman of the Child Psychiatric Committee, Southern California Psychiatric Society, Los Angeles, Calif.

Martha F. Leonard, M.D., Associate Professor of Clinical Pediatrics, Yale Child Study Center, New Haven, Conn.
Gale Linn, Ll.B., Attorney at Law, Denver, Colo.
Gladys Natches, Ph.D., Psychologist, New York City.
Philip Nelson, Ph.D., Clinical and Consulting Psychologist, San Francisco and Denver.
Robert G. Patton, M.D., Pediatrician, San Francisco, Calif.
Gerda L. Schulman, M.A., M.S.W., Family Therapist, Associate Professor, Family Treatment, Hunter College, Adelphi College, New York City.
Leon Tec, M.D., Director, Midfairfield Child Guidance Center, Norwalk, Conn.
Lenore Terr, M.D., Child Psychiatrist, San Francisco, Member of the faculty, University of California Medical School
David Ulrich, Ph.D., Psychologist, Stamford, Conn.
John Wendt, Ll. B., Justice, Pitkin County, Aspen, Colorado.
Robert Williams, Ph.D., Chief of Community Health Services, Sonoma County, Sonoma, Calif.
Nancy Winston, M.S.W., Step Family Foundation, New York City.

Living in Step

•/•

Introduction: The Secret World of Step Relations

THERE WE WERE. And many of our friends were there also. We were involved deeply in families that weren't our families, and yet they had to be. We were, and we weren't. We could, and we learned we shouldn't. We were somewhere between the fantasy and the facts of living in step.

Among us, we found a recurring dream, the dream of having a great big happy family. We found stepfamilies that other people believed were great big happy ones, but when we talked with the individual members we discovered their disappointments, their resentments, their tears. Sadly, we found all too few stepfamilies that were effectively dealing with the problems of living in step.

We were not either.

We were behaving and feeling in ways we hadn't planned. "Others" were treating us in ways we'd never experienced before. The effect of even our smallest effort had now become unpredictable. Love often produced unexpected hostility. And, on top of all this, there were these absent invisible people making decisions in our family lives.

Ruth was the first to remarry. Her new husband had three boys; she had one. Before Jeannette remarried three years later she thought Ruth was merely exaggerating or doing something wrong. After she remarried, out sprouted similar feelings and problems. She had one son and married a man with four girls. As the two of us talked and shared problems of living in step that had been troubling us, we began to suspect that there was some force operating in our families that was bigger than our own individual frustrations or inverted hopes. We decided to write this book.

We write it not as experts but as women who have experienced the problems of step and are looking for more and better explanations and solutions. We had prepared for our own children in our first marriages with extensive reading, and we believe nature has provided us with a natural receptivity. Both of us went blissfully into second marriages involving other children. Both were totally unprepared.

It had seemed simple enough. "I love you: I'll love your children." It wasn't.

We discovered that the difficulties of step relationships are handled primarily by denial that there is any problem. Neither parents, nor children, nor society is prepared to acknowledge the troubles endemic to the step situation. The dream of healing through remarriage persists. The new family will be just like the original one, only better. The old problems will disappear. That they will continue or that new problems will arise because of the very formation of the new family is not an idea that is easily tolerated.

The U.S. Bureau of Census tells us that it takes an average of 3 years for the remarriage to occur. The average marriage lasts for 7 years. The Bureau of Census goes on to tell us that the divorce rate is soaring. Right now New York ranks third in the nation behind California and Texas. In New York State *one out of every two marriages* ends in divorce. In the U.S. in 1974 there were 970,000 divorces with an average of 1.22 children per divorce.

We estimate, conservatively, there are *15 million children under 18 living in step families* and another *3-4 million between 18 and 22* living in and out of the immediate step family. We estimate that there are, at a minimum, *25 million husbands and wives* who are *stepmothers or stepfathers.*

In addition, we further estimate another 5-10 million married and divorced adults contemplating and wondering about what a remarriage with children would be like.

Everybody living in step relationships, whether full or part time, knows the problems. Nobody talks about it. Concurrently it is not being dealt with. Somehow the subject is taboo. It is defiling motherhood or apple pie, or the flag to admit that we have married again (we are used merchandise, not brand new) and not all of the children are ours. They just came as part of the deal. And, for many it is hard to acknowledge that the children are the worst part of the deal . . . that often we feel that dealing them out would be the nicest thing that could happen.

The stepfamily might be considered analogous, psychologically, to what happens physically in organ transplants. The most common cause of failure in transplants, as we know, is quite simple: the body responds protectively and rejects foreign tissue. Medical measures are taken to keep this from happening. Psychologically, the danger of similar pathology exists in the merged family situation.

The stepfamily brings with it foreign and inexperienced ways of communicating within groups of people. At the same time, the relationships are tender and tenuous. The comforts of the "never-go-away" constancy of the biological family are not present. Thus the demands for solutions are more crucial.

On the positive side, the stepfamily has in its favor the strength and effort inherent to all new ventures. The parents may also have a kind of second sight derived from prior experience.

In interviewing for this book we found an urgent poignancy in the point of view of each member of the stepfamily. Stepmothers poured out to us their feelings of being used and used and used. Stepfathers spoke of feelings of being strangers in their homes. Stepchildren described feelings of somehow never really belonging and at the same time being tugged in separate directions. Biological parents with children living with them in stepfamilies spoke of feeling split between children and mate. Absent parents communicated their sense of eroding loss and powerlessness over their children's development.

According to experts with whom we talked, it is only natural that conflict exists in every direction in the recently formed stepfamily. The love between the two newly married is precious and guarded; the other's children stand as a symbol of the old marriage, the old love. The stepparent cannot help resenting a "new" child as an obstacle or diminishment to the new marriage. Even should he or she love and accept the child, the child himself has his own mother or father, dead or alive, to whom he feels his primary loyalty. He cannot help resenting the intruder. The new family unit is assailed by ambivalent feelings and behavior—a great deal of which, once acknowledged and understood, can be dealt with.

Problems we believed to be particular and individual, we learned, were actually pervasive and predictable in stepfamilies. The heartaches are genuine, the elements multiple and unexpected, creating that ugly feeling we hate to admit in terms of the family—resentment. But the resentments are there. They are endemic to the stepfamily and are to be anticipated. Awareness of their roots allows the stepfamily to move forward.

RUTH ROOSEVELT
JEANNETTE LOFAS
July, 1975

1

In the Beginning: Hard Facts and Expectations

Beginning the step marriage is difficult at best—particularly when you expect it not to be. We looked forward to our new families with excitement. It would be like the implied happy beginnings that follow the endings of love stories and films. Basking in the warmth of male-female love, we were blissfully unaware of the jarring facts of the stepfamily.

What happens when you move from the role of friend and lover to that of spouse and stepparent? As one stepparent put it, "It's like being plunked down, a stranger, in the middle of rural China, speaking the wrong language and yet torn all the while by too many people asking unanswerable questions."

The most pervasive myth in a step marriage is that the stepfamily should function as does a natural family. It doesn't. Classic mistake number one is to think that it will. It can't.

THE CHILDREN ARE NOT YOURS

The children are not yours. And they never will be. In the traditional sense of marriage, the partner with prior children is not totally yours—and never will be. One of the hardest things to accept is that somebody else always has a prior claim to that spouse or that child.

The fact of the previous commitments and past history, always there, are continually being awakened. "I feel two ways about my stepchildren," one stepmother told us. "On the one hand, I care for them almost as if they were my own. On the other hand, I resent them, for they remind me of something I don't want to be reminded about."

One stepfather was particularly candid. He laughed and said, "I like the kids as people all right. I just resent the fact that they exist."

The additional demands of the other's children somehow feel like too much in the stepfamily. Biological parents naturally give and allow. Stepparents in the same situation may feel imposed upon. Biological parents hardly expect thank-yous in a parenting role. Stepparents by virtue of their outsider status need communicated appreciation to validate their efforts. They seldom get it.

For whatever came automatically to the child in the biological family he is now expected to be appreciative. He is expected to say thank you. In a sense, he has lost his birthright.

Children who desperately try to turn a stepparent into a natural parent can only be disappointed. Parents, as well, who eagerly try to replace a child's natural parent can also only be disappointed. As harsh as it sounds, no matter how great the effort, neither the stepparent nor the stepchild will ever achieve the kind of priority, or love, that the natural parent or child achieves. The love may be there; it will never be the same. That is the heartache, and the way, of step.

Nevertheless, the tendency is to expect, act, and react as though the stepfamily were a biological family. We have no other patterning.

A common complaint of those entering the secret (untalked-about) world of step is that relationships changed after the marriage, that right from the start things were much harder than anticipated. Janice, a close friend of ours, described to us the beginning of her step marriage:

JACK AND JANICE

She simply didn't understand it. Janice had been so close to Jack's children before they were married: long conversations, intimacies exchanged, laughter and giggles. Jack had said many times, "You're marvelous with my girls. They tell you far more than they've ever told me."

Then at the wedding Babs had cried; and Janice had thought it was because of the beauty of the ceremony. She and Jack had written it themselves. Even before hugging her son Andy, she'd gone running over to the girls to hug them and kiss them, saying, "Now I have the daughters I've always wanted." They pulled back.

That was the beginning. Marriage, tender love, long delightful nights of conversation and warmth. Then would come Sunday. Jack's three girls would come in the late afternoon and stay for dinner. The wonderful big family gatherings that Janice had dreamed about didn't happen.

Janice would spend practically the whole day preparing for them, cooking and so forth. By the time they'd arrive, she would be all keyed up inside.

Andy was so excited at the prospect of being part of a large family that he'd overact, overdo everything. When he wouldn't be noticed, he'd go from unruliness to whining. Often, after a few reprimands from Jack, he'd slink off to his room and watch television alone.

From the first, things seemed to go wrong. The girls were distant and cool, sometimes barely even saying hello to Janice or her son, Andy. Her efforts at conversation were responded to in monosyllables. They hid behind magazines and newspapers. It was as though they didn't even want to look at Janice or Andy.

One of those early Sundays she really blew it. First, she insisted they say hello to Andy. Then, she asked them to help her serve the dinner. Jack said they didn't have to help. She served the dinner alone, feeling like a servant. Before she even got all the plates on the table, heads were bent over, slurping up food. Some were practically finished before she sat down. Nobody looked at her, and nobody said anything to Andy.

"That's it!" She slammed her fist on the table. "Couldn't you at least have waited until we were all served?"

"That's the way we do it," Jack said. "The food will get cold, and besides they're hungry."

Janice couldn't help it. She started a total tirade about the difference between dining and eating. She suggested that next time they put their plates on the floor and eat with the dog.

Carefully the girls stared at their plates and forcefully moved the food into their mouths. Fork to mouth. Fork to plate. And back again. Arms working like pistons. As soon as they could, they left. Linda slammed the door.

Janice and Jack had a free-for-all attacking each other's children. Why had he defended them and not her? Why had she jumped on them? They hadn't done anything wrong. Didn't she have the perception to tell they were shy? And her sissy son with his weird noises. Wouldn't he ever stop whining? His stupid daughters showed no breeding whatsoever. Why did she keep babying that kid of hers? You and yours. No. Yours and you. Uproar. Then silence and separateness. What was happening to their love?

THE FINE TUNING REQUIRED

Like most of us entering the world of step, Jack and Janice expected too much, too soon, and knew too little about the fine tuning required to make a stepfamily work.

Like Jack and Janice, a couple may be blissfully in love, feeling able to move mountains or leap tall buildings in one single bound, only to be brought down by a child, and the loved spouse's reaction to an incident.

Of the many people we have spoken with who are professionally involved with family problems, nearly all advise premarital counseling for a couple about to remarry into a step situation. In step everyone needs help—yet 99 percent of remarrying couples don't, and probably won't, seek it.

Expectations run high. And so do disappointments. It's not hard to see why magic is so often expected from a second marriage. Having gotten out of a difficult relationship, having possibly been through a tough period of single parenthood, husband and wife expect wonders of the new marriage.

Far from taking a hard look at the inevitable problems and complications of a step marriage, the two adults are likely to have encouraged each other in their expectations. Promises, expressed or implied, of a loving marriage and of good parenting are part of the courtship dance. A father remarrying *expects* his new wife to be a wonderful mother. A mother remarrying *expects* her husband to be a strong and helpful father.

The children too may have been led to expect marvelous wonders from the new parent. Rosy pictures may have been vividly painted. Sometimes it is the children alone who know better. Sometimes they too believe, only to be let down. In any event, whatever the expectations, all too frequently the children test for the worst and do their level best to stir it up. Or they tie themselves up into knots, trying to bring about that "best" they were promised.

We also carried with us into our second marriages the joy and burden of high expectations.

THE MYTH OF INSTANT LOVE

It bewilders us now, yet indeed we were captured by the myth of what Gerda Schulman calls "instant love." I love you: I'll love your children. You love me: your children will love me. Somehow each member of the stepfamily feels he is expected to love and expects to be loved, *instantly*. To ascertain the fantasy, each tests the other, hoping for affirmation, yet fearful it won't be there.

From the beginning of the new union, each member is uncertain of his place in the new family structure. Jockeying for position, he seeks sure footing on new turf.

In the original marriage the merger was gentle. The couple awaited the child that later came to them. There was time. By contrast, in the stepfamily the merger of the children into the marriage is immediate. Many individuals are involved. The kinetics of displacement in the combined family cause feelings of uncertainty, a lack of belonging, and a not knowing where one's place is. Just as you've found your seat, somebody else sits down on it. Again and again it happened with us and ours and theirs.

Any change in family structure, even a prolonged visit of a grandparent to a natural family, will cause realignment struggles. How much more restructuring is involved in remarriages with children! All of the family members are part of the change in family structure. Each endeavors to belong somehow without losing any of his or her prior identity, whether it be as lover, mother, father, or child.

PLANNING THE MERGER

In the merger of two companies, careful plans are laid for the realignment of possessions, offices, duties, responsibilities. In the newly merged family the setting in order of people and things must be just as carefully planned. It's important that the couple discuss *beforehand* the structures and procedures, and how the authority for carrying them out is to be shared. Few of us can be comfortable in an environment in which everybody has a different way of doing things.

It helps greatly if the new family can start out in a new house. Planning for the house, where things are to go, who is to have what space, involves the whole family in the new adventure and adds a feeling of belonging. It is one of the most satisfying ways to go from "mine" and "yours" to "ours." When it is necessary to stay in one of the original homes, those who move in may not feel they belong; and those who move over may feel dispossessed.

A friend of ours talked about growing up in a single-parent household. Later in her life her mother remarried and moved to her new husband's house. By this time the daughter had an apartment in the city, but she often visited her mother and stepfather on weekends. In their new house there was not a room for her. Somehow she felt that she had to remove all her things after each visit. She didn't know why, but for years, although she was happy for her mother, she hated that marriage, that house. There was no place for her.

We all must belong. So must our possessions. Should the stepchildren come but once a month, allow them a drawer or a place for their things. Consider how much more like home a place feels if there's a drawer with your pajamas in it. It's like visiting strangers if you have to bring everything every time.

Little things like that can make all the difference in whether a child feels part of the family, or left out. Feeling left out can evoke some ornery behavior indeed, and often justly so. If a stepparent feels that there "isn't enough room" to provide a child with a space or room of his own, it may be important to examine the source of this feeling. (One stepmother gleefully admitted, after having the kids for the summer, to the pure pleasure of putting all their things in boxes and stashing them in a back corner of the attic the minute they left.) Whatever the feelings, the stepparent concerned about improving relationships within the family should consider whether or not visiting stepchildren have, literally, enough space.

Physical space helps. Clear and distinct rules of the house —agreed upon beforehand—can provide a road map for the new family. For example, in this house we say hello and goodbye, good morning and good night. Dinner is at seven. Wait to eat until everybody is served. This week Sarah and Charlie do the dishes. Stacey sets the table and takes out the garbage. Bedtime is a certain time for certain age groups. Everybody makes his bed and straightens his room before leaving in the morning. Everybody is responsible for his own homework, and he does it when he first gets home, etc., etc.—whatever fits the agreed-upon style and needs of the family as a whole and of the family members as individuals.

Agreed-upon courtesies oil the way and make it possible for strangers in step to become compatible family members. Rules of the house are not, necessarily, value judgments: one way is not right and another wrong. They are an agreed-upon *modus operandi* which makes it possible for children to live at various times in different homes and accept the different ways of each. They know where they are and can then adjust to the differences.

Rules of the house also solve the problem of, "My mom lets me do it." A simple statement—"In this house we do it this way"—resolves the impasse.

An example would be: "Your mother lets you stay up till midnight on Saturdays, and I'll bet you enjoy that. Well, in this house children your age go to bed at eleven on Saturday nights, so it's eleven for you tonight."

It's all a case of doing as the Romans do in Rome or the Smiths do at the Smiths' house. It makes getting along easier.

The rules of a healthy family, while consistently enforced, should not be rigid and unbendable. Frustration and rebellion can occur where rules cannot be altered to fit changing needs. (Dinner cannot be at seven for Suzie if she has play rehearsal at six-thirty.) The rules-of-the-house concept nonetheless remains a good one—all the better for a little flexibility.

THE SUPER STEPPARENT

Again and again, we have been advised that the way to initiate the stepparent role is *slowly*. Beginning the step marriage is a sensitive business. One scarred stepfather put it this way: "It has to be approached the same way that porcupines make love . . . v e r y   c a r e f u l l y !"

A fifteen-year-old boy with both a stepmother and a stepfather says, "You have to ease into it. It's sort of a strange relationship. Here is this other person, and they're coming into your life whether you like it or not. And you're going to get along with them whether you like it or not. Because you have to. I think it should be made as easy as possible because if people come on too strong, you just can't handle it."

New stepparents, especially stepmothers, often come on like superparents. They rush in with goodies, avowals of love, and excessive displays of parenting. They work so hard it spoils all the fun.

For some personalities, this is almost predictable, even irresistible. There is the enthusiasm for the new marriage, the desire to prove onself with one's mate—and to win over the children. There is the wish to compete successfully with the prior mate. And frequently, because of a belief (often mistaken) that the prior mate is a terrible parent, there is the desire to make up to the children for whatever they may have missed.

The counterpart of the super-stepparent (or stepchild) who tries zealously to make the new merger work is the stepperson who pulls back or withdraws. He or she may feel that no action is better than the wrong action, or withdrawal may be his way of dealing with a stressful situation. Having experienced one failure, he may be afraid of another and deal with the fear by holding everything in. Or he may be simply uninterested or disliking. Whatever the motive, the pulling away is most often interpreted as rejection in the sensitive world of step.

Super-stepparenting is the more common mistake. The stepparent, by trying to be a superparent, steps right into the sacred territory that the stepchild has reserved for his own mother or father (living or dead) and thereby activates his conflict of loyalties. The child cannot help pulling back and pushing away the super-stepparent. The super-stepparent cannot help being offended.

From the beginning both the needs and the behavior of the two are out of synchronization. The stepparent wishes to move (assertively) forward; the stepchild wishes to move (gingerly) backward. Later, the stepchild may be ready to accept stronger stepparenting. All too frequently, the stepparent by this time has been discouraged into retreat. Now it is the stepchild's turn to feel hurt.

CAROLINE

Taking it easy brings rewards. One woman who enjoys an excellent relationship with her stepchildren can't give the "reasons" for it—which may well be the "reason" in itself. "I didn't do anything special," Caroline says. "We just sort of went along."

She was twenty-four when she married a widower with two girls, aged eight and nine. She wasn't particularly excited about having the girls, she didn't especially want to be a mother, but she did want to marry their father.

Caroline treated the girls pretty much as she would any other person living in her house. She'd never been a mother, didn't have much experience with children, but she did remember how things had been done when she was a girl.

"You took baths, washed your hair, and dressed a certain way for school. You went to bed at a certain time, and you cleaned your room. You had some manners; you were polite to people."

She set up the rules as best she could, without worrying over whether the girls liked the rules or not. Nor did she worry about whether they liked or loved her—or anything. "Let's just go along," she'd say.

The girls were crazy about Caroline. It was they who initiated all the affectionate family steps. It was she who needed time to get used to being a mother. Because she did not push, the girls could set the pace.

Probably you will have noticed that Caroline's expectations weren't very high. We weren't as cool as Caroline. We know now that when the partners in a remarriage continue to have unrealistic expectations that one or both of them will be super-parents, the results can be disastrous. Good stepparenting is not at all the same as good parenting. Super-stepparenting can be counted on to foul up the works.

Often stepparents upset their new families in an effort to define immediately their own way of doing things in the home. They ask spouse and children to behave quite differently from the way they behaved before. They appear to be insensitive to the way things used to be.

We have found most rewarded those stepparents who realize that they must gradually build a bridge to their stepchildren. They realize that changes will come in time if they don't force them, and they arrive more quickly at their goals.

MARRYING A WIDOWER

Take the case of the stepmother who marries a widower and moves into his already established household. As she sets about making her own place in this house, she often tries to ensure her position by trying to eradicate that of the former wife.

It is important for the new wife to accept the fact that somebody did live here before and occupy the same space. This man did have a wife, and the place of that wife might as well be acknowledged. The woman who insists that all traces of the former wife be removed from the house and from memory is saying, "If you must have reminders of your first marriage, then you are not acknowledging your marriage with me." By forcing the family to choose when no choice is necessary, she invites resentment and resistance.

A wise stepmother will allow the stepchild the room that child needs for the memory of his mother. She will try to find a gentle way to reach out to the child, no matter how antagonistic—or frightened—that child may be.

HELENE

Helene, a stepmother with a very young stepdaughter who would barely speak to her, found a picture of the child's dead mother. She had it framed and gave it to the little girl. Together they found a place for the picture in the child's room. She spoke to the child about her loss, about how much the child must miss her mother.

"You know, the heart has a lot of sections," she said, "and it grows while you grow. There will always be a section of love in your heart for your mommy that will never go away. But you have other sections in your heart, for the love you have for your daddy and your sister and brother. As you grow older you will learn to love other people too, and there will be even more sections in your heart."

After that conversation the child started warming to Helene.

Unlike Helene, most stepparents make the mistake of trying to push the child to recognize their parenting role. In order to do this, they may want the child to dismiss the now absent or dead parent. The child simply cannot. Even if the parent is alive and flagrantly neglecting the child, the child cannot admit it. The continued belief in his parent is essential to his self-esteem. On the other hand, recognition of the role the stepparent is now playing is also vital to the self-esteem and continued efforts of the stepparent. The two meet in a sad deadlock, until parents, stepparent, and child grow toward making room for what was and what now is, excluding neither the past nor the present.

What any new situation needs is time. Time to become fully acquainted with a new house, a new mate, and new children.

Being a good stepparent requires a combination of knowing when to be active, when to take a moving, guiding role, and when to sit back, accept, be cool. Only then can you roll with the punches, recognize why they come and where they come from, and go with them.

This means involving yourself so much, but no more. Steering clear here, and moving in there. Restraining the natural instincts and yet meeting the extraordinary obligations of step.

2

Adjusting

MOST OR ALL members of the reconstituted family have lived through considerable trauma: the breakup of the family through separation, death, or divorce. Comes remarriage, and difficult adjustments are required at a time when family members —especially children—are likely to be psychologically tender, particularly prone to irrational behavior.

The loss of the original family is reawakened in the child and magnified by the addition of a new stepparent. The child's resentment of this loss-and-replacement may focus on the new stepparent. Surface behavior—too often taken at face value—can be confusing indeed. An example is the story a friend told us about his five-year-old stepson Johnny.

Johnny and his new stepfather had finished raking leaves into a big pile for Johnny to jump into. Suddenly Johnny turned to his stepfather and said, "I want to live with my real daddy, not with you."

The stepfather put down the rake and went inside. That night at dinner Johnny's mother was dismayed by his coldness toward her son.

Johnny, however, in his need to test and inquire, may well have been asking his stepfather, "Will you like me for a long time? Is it fair to my daddy that I like you? Will I lose my daddy if I love you?"

Here the behavior of the stepchild initiated a parallel response on the part of the stepparent, for he too was vulnerable and uncertain.

The original incident was compounded when Johnny's stepfather came home the following night and found mother and son engrossed in play. He received only the most perfunctory of greetings, and for the rest of the evening felt like an outsider. And so the colors of discontent began to thicken. All too often, at this point, stepfamilies become involved in a spiral of hostility, resentment, and withdrawal, much of which could be avoided.

Such dissatisfaction is augmented by confusion. Who we are, what we are doing, and how each of us feels about the others are hard to clarify in step. Perceptions are frequently distorted, leading to inappropriate behavior. The process of idealization goes awry, and misplaced feelings abound.

IDEALIZATION

Idealization simply doesn't operate in step the way it does in the ordinary family. There, it is natural for most parents to idealize their children. After all, the child is the extension of the parents' own ego, the extension of themselves. To them, any accomplishment that is the least bit special may be considered extraordinary. Together they dote on the child. As time passes, their idealization becomes tempered with reality, but the presumption usually remains in the child's favor.

In the development of the healthy child, doting love serves a valuable psychological function. This positive reinforcement, this being believed in almost unconditionally, helps the child develop self-esteem, the crucial building block to personality. It leads to confidence as he sizes up his own chances of achievement in life.

Children also idealize their parents. ("My daddy is the strongest." "My mommy is beautiful.") They also, in their way, dote. The idealization of their parents adds to their self-picture. ("It's true because my mother said so.") As children grow older, they continue to idealize in a more subtle and sophisticated way.

Healthy doting and idealization build family loyalty, which in turn makes a family a sanctuary, a safe harbor for growth. Should any member trip up in life, the family will be there supporting him.

Stepparents and stepchildren don't dote, at least not over

their stepchildren and stepparents. Competitive domination rather than support may be the prevailing attitude. Indeed, things may reach such proportions that, should any family member trip, the misstep may be looked upon with glee by the others.

SEEING THINGS DIFFERENTLY

Stepparents see things differently than natural parents. This perceptual difference can be helpful. They can be more objective, better able to identify problems of the stepchild that biological parents may not recognize or be willing to face. On the other hand, stepparents can undermine a child by being hypercritical. In any case, a stepparent and a biological parent look at the same child from totally different perspectives. Each may accuse the other of distorted interpretations of a child's actions. Each may be right. In step, the biological parent often instinctively tries to preserve the level of idealization in the original family, sensing that this is vital to the child. The result is often irritating to the stepparent. ("You spoil your children." "You don't see their faults." "You overindulge yours.")

There is something more than idealization that goes on. Certain defense mechanisms can keep step people from recognizing deficiencies in themselves or their biological family members and somehow attributing the faults to their step relations. It results in a kind of whitewashing or building up on the one side and a tarring or tearing down on the other side—a tandem see-sawing distortion of perceptions.

TRANSFERRING BAD FEELINGS

Two of the defense mechanisms are called projection and displacement of feeling. Displacement is the process through which an emotion or feeling is unconsciously transferred from its source (for example, a mother) to a more acceptable substitute (for example, a stepmother). A child who seems furious with his stepfather or stepmother may in fact be deeply angry with his biological mother or father. Since the process of displacement is unconscious, he is, of course, unaware of the real source of his anger.

Here's how it works. A child in a stepfamily whose mother or father is absent and neglecting may feel a strong need to cover up for that missing parent. He needs to believe that his parent has not failed him. (My parent cannot love me.) He's hurt, frightened, and angry, yet he can't allow himself to believe that a person on whom he is or has been dependent for survival can behave in such a manner. He copes with his anxiety by placing the feelings elsewhere. Frequently, the stepparent bears the brunt—it is, after all, less hurtful inside to be angry or disappointed with the stepparent than with one's very own parent.

Projection is another defense mechanism often at work in the stepfamily. In projection a person attributes his own feelings or wishes to someone else because he can't take responsibility for these feelings or tolerate the painful effects they evoke. For example, a stepparent who feels hatred for a stepchild might find it more comfortable to convince himself that it is the stepchild who hates, thus relieving himself of responsibility for the ugly emotion and protecting his self-image.

The step situation provides multiple targets for displaced feelings and projections, which may come out in lines of dialogue like these:

"I hate my stepfather. He's really mean to me. If I were living with my dad, none of this would happen."

"If it weren't for your bratty kid, we'd get along."

"If he didn't have to pay so much alimony, everything would be okay."

"If it weren't for your ex-wife, we both could do so much better with these kids."

"My child would be all right if it weren't for his step (mother, father, sister, brother)."

Steppeople loaded down with misdirected feelings struggle along under a burden that can't get lighter. If the anger or disappointment were accurately directed and discharged, there would be release. Without this, new causes for dissension are created.

A stepchild who blames a stepparent for a parent's neglect

can easily create a situation in which he will be neglected not only by his parent but by his stepparent as well.

There it is for the stepperson. The seemingly excessive idealization of the natural family member; the seemingly unfair blaming of the stepfamily member. Unearned good image. Unearned bad image.

Idealization, displacement, projection, and the resulting ambivalence and resentment—all these can work simultaneously in the stepfamily, often without any apparent reference to the actual situation. In the stepfamily all of this is intensified.

SEEING EACH OTHER AS SYMBOLS

Instead of looking at each other as individuals, all too often steppeople see each other as symbols. Each person is perceived or experienced as a symbol of somebody else or some other commitment. Viewing the others as symbols, we feel that we ought to go about loving when we don't. Assessing the others as symbols, we often go about disliking when we really don't. That woman is where my mother belongs. That man is where my father should be. Those children are the product of an alien and prior love: they dilute the loyalties to this love and marriage. When we look at somebody as a symbol, we evoke predetermined emotions and counter emotions.

WHAT'S IN A NAME

The choosing of "titles" is a psychological as well as a practical problem in step. How the problem is resolved provides an indicator of the child's adjustment to the new family.

"I'm your new mother" is almost certain to evoke instant recoil. One thirteen-year-old put the response succinctly: "The hell you are."

Another stepchild says: "I had a stepfather. It took me two years to call him Dad. Mother often said, 'You know Robert would be so happy if you'd call him Dad.' I wouldn't. I couldn't for a long time, even though he was kind and I knew from Mother that it would make him happy. Then one day two years after they were married, I tried it . . . 'Dad.' The room just kind of stopped and warmed. Our relationship changed after that, too. He just did more fatherly things."

In our research we found families groping for acceptable names. Some families refer to the stepfather as Daddy John or Daddy Fred. The stepmother is called Mommy Jean or Mom Suzanne. Many more ask only for the use of the first name—"Call me Bruce," or "Call me Betty."

Many experts say that this informal nomenclature diminishes the authority of the stepparent, the adult. Others feel that the individual stepparent either does or doesn't have authority, that what he or she is called doesn't matter. Yet we do, all of us, respond and react differently to a person we address as Judge Adams than we do to one we call Hank. "Mom" and "Dad" being titles with extraordinary emotional clout, it seems particularly important that they not be forced on the stepchild before he or she is ready.

Many stepchildren have told us that they were asked right from the start to call their new stepparent Dad or Mom. Invariably they resented it. Sometimes, of course, it's the new stepparent who does not want to be called Dad or Mom, who may not be ready. Remember Caroline, the young woman without children who married the widower? When the children wanted to call her Mom, she said, "I'm new at this. Give me time."

They did. They gave her ten months, until Mother's Day. That day—along with the card—they said, "No more Caroline. Now you're Mommy." And that was that for the next twenty years.

The decision as to what to call stepparents is understandably difficult. In the title "Mother" or "Father" there is nothing to differentiate the biological parent from the stepparent. The titles "Stepmother" and "Stepfather" are so loaded with negative connotations that they amount to smear words.

THERE ARE NO EX-PARENTS

Anne Simon, in *Stepchild in the Family,* defines the problem:

> The modern family—so new and varied that it has as yet no definition—tries to fit step relationships to the old family form, symbolized by its names. The wish is destined for frustration.
>
> The child sees what adults don't want to see, that a man can have a new wife, a woman a new husband, but that he, the child, cannot have a new parent. There is no such thing as an ex-mother or ex-father. He has a parent, alive or dead, in his mind, and this new person is an impostor who wants to seize the only exclusive non-transferable word in the language . . . and the relationship that goes with it.

True, and yet we have seen stepchildren who long to call the stepparent Mom or Dad, but hesitate to do so because they are uncertain of the response. One little boy told his mother, "I want to call him Dad so bad the word sticks in my mouth."

Perhaps here a little encouragement from the natural parent is in order. Shyness or established family tradition may be keeping the child from using the title he longs to use. The parent can allow the child to do what he wants. It might be best, however, to find a title not identical to the one used to designate the natural parent. Here's how this worked out for one stepfather and stepdaughter.

"At first, she called me Daddy. Then, after a trip across the country to see her father, she came back not knowing what to call me. She was wrestling with the problem of who her father was, and what I was to her.

"I thought, well, her father's her real father. How do I make it simple for her? I didn't want in any way to make her problem worse. We had a heart-to-heart talk over what she should call me.

"Who was I? Was I her father? No. At the beginning of the marriage, I had offered my first name—both she and her mother had rejected that. Finally I said the best name is just what I am, *Stepfather.* For two years she called me that, though it was very awkward for her.

"All this finally resolved itself. She worked out another solution. She got tired of calling me Stepfather and her stepmother Stepmother. She asked if it was all right if she called me Poppa. Daddy was her real father.

"Well, Poppa was fine. I'm Poppa now."

Until a happy title is found, we feel it important to at least soften the current titles—"This is my stepmom, my stepdad." "This is John's son, my stepson, Bob"—with an "up" tone of voice. The tone we use in designating our step relationships is crucial. A bad word can be made light by an easy tone, as well as the reverse.

On the intimate family level, it's hard to find names and titles. As the family extends, it's easier. For example, it's easier to have a lot of grandparents. One does not displace the other—there are more than one of each to begin with. One family we know refers to the stepgrandparents as Grand Vicky and Grand Sam.

Why not? In all "title" situations, whatever is most comfortable (and unforced) for the child is likely to work out best.

DIFFERENT LIFE STYLES

An original family has time to build up a life style according to the traditions, needs, and personalities of its members. A stepfamily starts with different life styles. The range of what steppersons have to adjust to runs the gamut—from superficial annoyances to different scales of values.

For one stepmother the big adjustment was having to raise her voice when she was disciplining the children.

"Somebody had to do it before chaos took over," she told us. "My husband would sit reading a book, not even aware of the decibel level until it got so bad he'd be in a fury. What I disliked was not only having to do the disciplining, but having to do it in a loud voice. It didn't feel like me. I had grown up in a quiet family. In this family I have to scream sometimes in order to be heard."

Before remarriage, a stepparent's household may have been orderly and neat. The new family members drop things all over the house, walking across their own mess if need be. As one stepmother put it, "It seems as if the room begins to litter itself as soon as one of them walks through its door."

The problem may "only" be a matter of words. For an open and verbal stepfather, the hardest part can be adjusting to less-verbal, less-open children. Or it can be just the reverse: a quiet stepparent may feel overwhelmed by talkative children.

We understood how it was for one stepmother: The kids were always talking, talking, talking. Word after word hammering on her head. Their disparagements of whatever she was doing or was trying to do were so eloquent! By the time she'd get a silence in which to say something, the words had already left her. She felt shoved around by tides of talk, exhausted with the running of words.

In situations like these, according to Sidney Gerhardt, a Connecticut psychiatric social worker, the stepparents might just as well spend their energies adjusting instead of fighting the inevitable. New people and more people mean increased adjustment. "We go to our graves adjusting," says Gerhardt. "At least I hope I go to mine still adjusting."

THE SMITHS AND THE JONESES

The Jones and Smith families merge in a second marriage. The Joneses have wall-to-wall animals, easy patterns, superflexible rules, dinner whenever anyone is hungry. The Smiths have firm rules, set dinner hours, absolute bedtimes, and *no* animals.

Mrs. Jones (now Mrs. Smith) is permissive, forgiving, yielding on discipline. Mr. Smith establishes set rules, punishments, and expectations. He even spanks.

When things go awry, the Smith family harps, needles, and nags. The Jones family screams, stamps feet, and throws things.

Mrs. Smith (formerly Jones) remembers how it was in the beginning. She'd be standing in the kitchen with the older Smith girls, who would say, "Mom kept all the utensils neatly in the drawer," or "Yuk, the garbage is a mess," or "I gave you my dress last week to hem. Where is it?"

At the same time, Mrs. Smith's son, furious over something, would be throwing pots and pans on the floor.

She'd cringe at the dinner table while her daughter teased

the Smith girls for being virgins and regaled them with the wonders of sexuality. (She'd never heard this from her daughter before.)

Mrs. Smith recollects the hurt of those early years, and how she would talk to her own children and her husband about what was going on. Bit by bit they reached a level of mutual acceptance. They began to teach each other something.

The dowdy Smith girls began to take advice from their fashionable stepmother and were grateful for compliments they'd never gotten before. Mr. Smith's even temper and authority seemed to calm down the Jones children and give them some self-discipline.

Mr. Smith had never traveled outside the United States. Mrs. Smith was an inveterate globe trotter. He delighted in the newfound pleasure of travel with his wife. She welcomed his companionship and quiet strength. They shared with each other their worlds, and indeed each was enriched and expanded by the other.

"Soon you find yourself doing their things," says Ruth, "and enjoying it. I learned to play tennis to please the family. Soon I was the one who always, always wanted to play.

"They begin to do some of your things. For example, I love it when one of the boys delivers back to me an argument about something I want them to do or not to do. They are playing my game: talking it out. Often I let them win if they say it well. I have always loved an articulate rebellion.

"Over the years you find them somehow slipping into your type of thinking. Something you said six months ago that caused an argument you now hear them promoting as gospel. And you think, well, maybe their point was kind of right too. The mutual history begins. The merger develops its own character. Our particular combined family has developed its own style, its own jokes, its own manners, its own values. We also have developed our own solidarity."

The gulf of incompatibility can be crossed. Those of us who cross it have to move from difference to acceptance, with plenty of adjusting along the way.

3

The Stepmother: I Am and I Am Not

THE STEPMOTHER HAD had enough.

She had been an actress, admired and respected in her profession. Now she was a wife and stepmother.

It had gotten so that she'd wake up at 4:30 in the morning with so many resentments she hadn't dislodged. Boulders in the mind. She'd go over them and over them, one by one, like so many treasures. Her smooth, white hatreds.

She felt she was standing on the ruins of someone else's life, and paying, paying, paying for their past mistakes.

The children. Fighting, whining, and stealing from each other. Lying too. Every time she'd try to do something about it, their father would act as though it were she who'd done something wrong. "Stop picking on them," he'd say. Couldn't he see what they were like?

And why did they have to be so sullen with her? Sometimes they actually seemed to dislike her. She'd tried so hard. If that's what you got for trying, what was the point in continuing?

And their mother never once said thank you for all the summers and vacations she'd taken care of them. Not once. For that matter, neither had the kids. What did they all take her for, their personal servant?

The stepmother pushed her feet into the bed, tensed her hands, and held every joint firmly in its place. Then she shifted to a more comfortable position.

Those children seemed to think they had an automatic right

to everything without ever having to do anything themselves. They looked at it as some kind of one-way street. Maybe it was. It certainly seemed that way to her. Endlessly her husband would give to his first family.

And that was another point. Why did he pay child support for all those months the children were away from their mother? She took care of the kids, and the mother got paid for it. What about that? And he paid her alimony while she lived with other men. Why did he let her walk all over him?

The worst part of it was that her husband would never defend her. She yearned, at those times when the kids were being hostile or rude to her, to have him stand up to them and say, "This is my wife, whether you like it or not." But he wouldn't. He also would let his first wife say anything about her to the kids and never stop her. "I can't control what she does," he'd say. But let *her* say one word against the first wife! "You can't run down the children's mother to them," he'd say. Well, what about not running down the children's stepmother?

Why should she sit silent and let the kids resent her not buying them the clothes their mother was paid to buy them? Why wouldn't her husband just tell the children how much he paid their mother? Let them resent *her* for a change.

The more she did for them the worse things got. Maybe she should just stop. Let them resent their father, eat nothing but junk, practice lousy manners, and go around in filthy clothes. Damn it, she had too much pride for that. Besides, she really did care.

Shouldn't she at least be allowed to defend herself? The truth could never hurt children. Who was her husband protecting by enforcing silence? Not herself, that was for sure.

She noticed that she'd been holding her toes straight up; she relaxed them, wishing she could get to sleep.

The trouble with a second marriage is you never come first.

Then the idea came to her—slowly, bringing solace and release. A womanly springtime. She would have an affair with somebody. It would be something completely her own, something not somehow so secondhand.

Or, well, at least she'd take a trip alone. Get away. Leave her husband to take care of his own beloved children. Maybe then they'd appreciate her. She had to do something for herself.

So thinking, the stepmother fell asleep.

The stepmother can work herself into quite a state: resentful, frustrated, put-upon, and wanting (but not wanting) to break away. We meet her day after day in the grocery store; she will tell you over and over the same grievances, the same frustrations.

Or maybe she pretends that everything is fine, just fine. "We both consider all of the children as our own. There is no difference."

Perhaps she has a double list—of things she feels and of things she thinks she ought to feel.

Maybe she's an exception for whom everything *is* okay. Maybe.

THE PIVOTAL POSITION

Not only her mind is caught, she is caught. Usually she doesn't get away. Unlike the other members of the family, she often doesn't go to the office or school. Even when she does work, she remains responsible for the basic functioning of the family. She is, she sometimes feels, a sitting duck—a target for the angers and blows that can't go elsewhere.

The stepmother stands in a pivotal position. The family circles around her. In step the force of this position may be centrifugal, whirling the stepmother into confusion. As the woman of the house, she usually has the most power, and hence responsibility, in the formation of everyday family life. In step, however, that powerful center of the family may effectively be rendered powerless.

By the old traditions, her family, her marriage, are her primary concern. Yet they are not her family. They do not belong to her. As a mother she is in an unnatural role.

One part of her keeps acting as though she can make the family her own; indeed, as though it's her moral responsibility to do so. She often feels the need to simulate the emotions and behavior of a biological mother. She may even feel these emotions. But she can't expect a return—certainly not an early or easy return.

The force of conflicting emotions buffets her. Her instincts are severely curtailed. Should she overstep her territory, she may be shoved back to her "place." More often she complains that she doesn't quite know where her "place" is. Ruth in one of those moments wrote:

I am, and I am not.
I must be, and I may not be.
I have a job to do,
But I must not do it too well.

I am that sound of one hand clapping.
I play tennis without a ball and golf without a club.
In this game, they've changed all the rules.
And they never admit I'm playing.

Can I look at the flowers and never pick one?
Can I listen to the birds and never name one?
Can I raise all his children,
And never have his baby?

Don't tell me to draw the lines
And never cross beyond
To anger, and expectation, and love.
Hell, who do you take me for?

A BAD PRESS

A stepmother must, for her own self and for her family, unravel the myths of the stepmother. Could she become a cruel stepmother? Never! Well, the way things went today . . . Somewhere back there, where reasons and feelings come from, dark myths exist.

Even the smallest child has been indoctrinated through fairy tales depicting the wickedness and cruelty of stepmothers. The myths have been repeated so often that adults, as well as children, actually believe them. There must be some primal basis of truth, or the myths wouldn't have survived.

A hairdresser told this story: "When I was a little boy, I had a friend whose mother had died. I'll never forget the day his father returned home from his honeymoon with his new wife, the boy's stepmother. Three of us sat out behind the garage, dragging out all the stories we'd heard about stepmothers. We kept telling the poor kid worse and worse stories until we were all terrified.

"By the time the father arrived, we genuinely expected to see an ogre. When we heard his father calling him, we hid in the bushes. The father called and called, and finally the kid had to respond—was he scared!—and go in. We tried to look through the windows to see what she looked like, and what she was doing to him.

"She turned out to be a neat lady—she did far more for us than the other mothers on the block. But it took us the longest time to believe that underneath all that niceness something awful wasn't lurking. I can remember my mother saying, 'Imagine what this woman has taken on. Give her a break.' Still, it was months before we'd dare to eat the cookies that she baked for us."

THE FAIRY TALES

How did the image develop, and why has it persisted?

Simple, beautiful stories have captivated parents and children in all countries and times. A good, dear child—just like you—lost her wonderful mother to her grave and to heaven. Hard times came, for her good father married a wicked, wicked woman who made the little child's life so dreadfully hard. . . .

Fairy tales are enveloping experiences. Because of their extremes, they're emotionally satisfying. It's white and black all the way, the pure and the soiled, the wicked woman and the unspoiled child. The story is told from the child's point of view, and the child represents all humankind in its most innocent and vulnerable condition.

Rewards and punishments parallel heaven and hell. Being

eaten or locked up or left in the woods takes the place of hell. Heaven is having your father to yourself, or marrying a prince. All good, clean fun—except for the stepmother. She gets it in the end, but first she's shown to richly deserve the worst.

As we remember, Snow White's stepmother was a queen and had always been the most beautiful of them all. Snow White, however, had been growing prettier and prettier with every passing day. In the middle of a harsh winter the queen consulted her mirror; it told her that Snow White was now fairer than she. The stepmother could bear it no longer, and she had Snow White taken out to the woods to be put to death.

It was also out into the woods that a stepmother sent Hansel and Gretel. Without enough food to go around, something had to give. The stepmother thought it ought to be her husband's children. At first he couldn't quite go along with this, but the stepmother gave him no peace till he consented.

The most popular of all fairy tales is Cinderella. "Cinderella" has become a synonym for a deprived stepchild. Not sent away like Hansel and Gretel and Snow White, Cinderella is instead kept at home in dreadful old clothes doing all the dirty work. Her stepfamily, her father and stepmother and stepsisters dress up in fancy clothes and go off to the ball where there is to be a handsome prince, and leave her home alone.

There are other step fairy tales, even more extreme. In "The Juniper Tree" the stepmother cuts the stepchild up into pieces and makes a soup that she serves the father, who eats it.

Now here's an interesting point—the father in the fairy tales is never held culpable for his action or inaction. It is all the stepmother's doing; she alone bears the blame. As the most powerful human in these stories, she can be overcome only by supernatural forces.

It is shocking to note how powerless the father is. He is either absent, out of the picture, or present and the complete pawn of his wife. We do not hold him responsible. The villain is the stepmother.

FEELING OBLIGED TO LOVE

The presumption operates against the stepmother. She starts out with a mythical black eye and frequently goes on to earn a real one. Consciously or unconsciously, she nearly always tries to prove herself. She will *not* be a neglectful, depriving stepmother —yet her very efforts can create greater difficulties. Her stepchildren often cannot accept all her mothering and loving attentions. Acceptance feels too much like disloyalty to Mom, be she alive or dead. Since the stepmother's very existence alerts a conflict of loyalties in the stepchildren, she *is* in a sense culpable, decidedly the guilty party. Guilty if she does, guilty if she doesn't.

The "simple" matter of mother love is, in fact, a trap for the stepmother. She believes that she has an obligation to her husband (and to society, and perhaps even to God) to love her stepchildren. Both society and her husband do in fact expect it of her. Maybe even God does.

"Don't you love my children?" asked a concerned stepfather.

"Not yet, Roy," answered a stepmother who hadn't fallen into the trap.

To us she added, "They're not even the type of people I would choose for friends outside a family." So saying, she stated a harsh family fact: there are people we are connected to by blood that we don't especially like, and yet we are loyal and loving to them. What happens when the blood tie is missing?

Many feel the necessity to feign "blood" emotions. Feeling obligated to simulate mother love, a stepmother can feel guilt if she doesn't somehow miraculously and instantly feel actual unbiased love for her new and alien children. Nobody has told her that she doesn't have to feel love, that the extent of her moral imperative is to treat a child kindly as a human being.

Feeling obliged to love a stepchild and getting withdrawal sprinkled with hostility, a stepmother may tend to resolve the discrepancy by constructing an emotional brief of stepchild unlovableness. She lists and relists her stepchild's faults and inadequacies. Who, her thinking goes, could ever be expected to love this child? And she cancels her debt.

Driving a stepmother toward her stepchildren is her desire to extend her love for her husband to his children. She wants to succeed in her marriage; she feels she cannot tolerate another loss or failure. To secure her husband's love, she tries to make the children love her. Unconsciously she looks to the children to sanction her marriage—a mistake and a firm step into the trap.

Love cannot be forced any more than sexual attraction can be forced. Children have sensitive antennae to phoniness.

"I love you," says the stepmother.

"Bull shit," says the brave nine-year-old. "You don't even know me."

LOVE CAN HAPPEN

But love can happen, and it does. It is more likely to come when it is not expected, as one stepmother, Rachel, put it when she described the moment when love happened. Her life, she said, was both complicated and enriched by her love for her stepson.

"There came a point when he was in trouble with himself. At the time he was living with us only during the summer months. His father was away; I was horrendously busy with my work, feeling sorry for myself, and not paying much attention to him.

"One afternoon when I was trying to work, his problems kept coming back to me, again and again. I shoved the work aside, sat down on the bed, and cried as if my heart would break. 'God-damnit,' I thought, 'I *love* him!' His problems had become my problems.

"Then I considered what I could do to help him. I didn't know, then, whether or not he loved me. Later I found out that he did, but his feelings toward me weren't crucial at the moment. What was crucial was that I wanted to help him. Love had happened. Responsibility had happened."

Mutual love does happen, and it can be exhilarating. The successful stepmother, however, can crowd neither the child nor herself into love.

If she violates her stepchild's emotional boundaries, she will achieve not a return on her love but a reverse emotion. She cannot cross over into the holy land of mother love. If she offers too much, it will be fired back at her, bent and distorted.

THE DESIRE TO BE VALUED

Many a stepmother talks of wanting to be the real thing—to be the real wife, the real mother, at least the real stepmother. She wants to be validated in her role.

In first marriages, opposition often comes from the in-laws. In second marriages, the resistance comes from within the stepfamily itself.

The problem is particularly acute at the beginning. It is often exemplified by the children's reluctance to accept the new wife's new name. Ruth remembers being upset when early in her marriage one of her stepsons answered the telephone: "Mrs. Roosevelt isn't here. She's in Aspen." She remembers other times. Once when a salesperson said, "Here's your bread, Mrs. Roosevelt," another stepson said, "That's not Mrs. Roosevelt. That's Mrs. Anthony."

A disgruntling experience for any new wife, but especially upsetting to a new stepmother. From the child's point of view, this woman has not only married their mother's husband, she has now assumed their mother's name. In defense of his own, the stepchild's only recourse is to say, "No, you're not." If the stepmother realized the predictability of these feelings, she wouldn't take it so personally.

Something is working against her. The more she wishes to be authenticated, the more her stepchildren and others will seem to conspire to say no, that she is not it, not it at all. Outside the cast of central characters, she is not a major player.

In his play, *Lady from the Sea,* Ibsen has the stepmother say:

> In this house I have nothing to keep me. I have no roots here. The children are not mine. They don't love me. They have never loved me. . . . I haven't even a key to give up, or any instructions to leave behind. I have been outside—outside everything. From the first day I came here.

DEFINING THE POSSIBLE

The stepmother who attempts to play mother rather than stepmother can lose even these roles that are legitimately hers. Aspiring to the impossible, she loses the possible. "The problem," says Jeannette, "is defining what is 'the possible.' There *are* ways of handling this madness.

"In my case, I in no way endeavored to mother my stepchildren. They had a perfectly good mother at home and didn't need two as far as I was concerned. However, I admit to having had secret expectations and fantasies about becoming an admired female mentor in their lives.

"During my first marriage and before my second marriage, I'd worked as a journalist for twelve years. Now through my fairy godmother I was miraculously transformed into a full-time, nonworking, they-lived-happily-ever-after wife and mother and stepmother. I found that being a full-time working mother was nowhere as difficult as being a part-time stepmother.

"I remember those first few weekends of our marriage, the days Bob's girls would come to stay. Even now I feel it in my stomach. For thirty-odd years I'd lived with a cast-iron stomach. Nothing upset it, not even cotton candy, hot dogs, rollercoasters, or small planes in hurricanes. Nothing, but nothing, bothered my stomach.

"Early Saturday mornings I'd begin to feel sick, like I was pregnant or something. I was pregnant all right, with fear and a heavy implantation of resentment.

"They would come in and hardly say hello. I would reach out to them; they would walk away. I would hug them; they would stiffen. I would speak; they would say little or nothing. They got me where it hurt the worst. The more I talked, the less they responded.

"It took me a while to realize that what I had failed to do was to look for the cause of my stepchildren's actions. I simply wasn't aware at the time that these girls had suffered a severe loss when Bob and I had become husband and wife. They could never actually lose their father, but in actual time and attention they had indeed lost a good part of him—to me. Without wanting it or knowing it, we were catapulted into a game of emotional Capture the Flag. The prize, Bob. To whom would he show loyalty? With whom would he side?

"Lucky girls, to be getting me—and Lars, the little brother I knew they had always wanted? Not as far as they were concerned. I was something they had to put up with in order to see their father. Now I wasn't Jeannette, the fun friend; I was Jeannette, the usurper of their father. Neither they nor I could articulate these feelings at the time, but they let me have it, the brunt of their emotions, without even an explanatory note.

"And their father, my love, my prince charming, the man to whom I had plighted my troth and for whom I had thrown away my girl-reporter badge—what did he do? Nothing. They attacked me, and he quietly listened as they tore every feather from my crown. They were impolite, rude, and emotionally crude. Should I defend myself, he would take *their* side. For the first time in my life I was tongue-tied. Disbelieving what was going on, I sat stymied, too afraid to speak. Should I let that anger out, it would surely disembowel our new marriage.

"Once, after they had left, I attempted to talk with my husband about it. I struck out. I got nowhere in the battle of my-children your-children. They were no problem, he said—*I* was the problem. For the first time in my adult life I really felt helpless. What had I gotten myself into? I'd rather interview the President, cover a plane crash, have seventeen for dinner than spend those lonely days trying to figure out how I could manage this job of mother, stepmother, and wife.

"Well, it took about three weeks. I typed memos in quadruplicate, tore them up, finally picked up the telephone. I asked the two oldest to come up to the house one weekday after school. I wanted to talk to them alone, without their dad. They came. I was determined not to fire off my anger at them, but to get them to understand where I was at.

"It was probably the wisest move I ever made on the level of interpersonal relationships. More than two years later I still have the notes made prior to that meeting. (I had prepared for it as any good reporter would prepare for an interview.)

"They walked in the door with their eyes cast on the floor, as though there were something to be found there. I said little, none of the usual How are you, What's happening at school, etc. I allowed moments to pass, no longer rushing. It was my time now to say my piece. I began slowly.

" 'I know it's a difficult time for you children . . . problems between your father and your mother. It's hard having your dad's new wife around, and your mom's new husband. I bet you feel left out a lot. I feel left out a lot myself. I'm aware that there are problems for you—but there are problems for me too.'

"I made it very clear that I had no intention of taking their father from them, that the house was always open to them. I explained that I perceived their behavior as lack of interest in me and my son, as rudeness, as ill-mannered. That I felt offended. 'For example, when you call, you just ask, "Is Dad there?" No "Hi, Jeannette, how are you?" You've used the only weapon I can't deal with,' I told them, 'and that is your back. You've turned your back on me, ignored me, walked away from me. It hurts.

" 'Never once since the marriage have you asked me about me or mine or what I was doing. It's always been me doing the work, talking to you, and trying to discover what you were doing and feeling.

" 'I've got to tell you right now, one human being to another, that I'm very angry about it.

" 'I offer you a new start. We can sit here, we can talk. Or we can use your favorite weapon and go and turn our backs on each other. I say the choice is yours.'

"Silence. The beautiful blond-haired second-oldest began to cry quietly, saying nothing as I went on. Then the oldest, saying, 'Yes, it's difficult for us. We're just not good at communicating. Even some of our friends tell us we're hard to talk to. . . .'

"I had brought them both to tears, or perhaps just allowed their tears. I moved over uneasily and sat between them. We hugged each other like children. I don't to this day remember whether I cried or not. We all had a lot to cry about. But now at least it was there in front of us. We could be accountable or aware, should more of these I-wish-you-were-not-here transactions go on between us.

"This one episode did *not* bring the whole story to a happy ending. But a step in step had been made. It was a step to openness and acceptance of our feelings—and a clear delineation of what I couldn't and wouldn't take from them."

BEING AN OUTSIDER

Every stepmother, no matter what the family setup is, has to face the problem of being an outsider.

One stepmother told us that she was never included in family conferences. The mother and father would keep her uninformed about the children's needs and problems. And yet it was she who was left with the children much of the time.

One summer when she had the children she was not told that one of them was having difficulty learning to read and that the school had advised summer tutoring. She had been a reading teacher and was well equipped to give the child some help.

The parental couple drew boundaries to exclude her, thereby refusing to validate her in her role as stepmother. The others, however, may have been unable to include her. They may have wanted to hide family weaknesses. They may have felt threatened by her abilities and interest.

In this case the stepmother was really asked to step back—to not do what she could do well, to allow them the time necessary to accept her and her abilities.

The role of the stepmother obviously varies depending on the amount of time the children are with her and their father and upon the degree of involvement of the mother and father. There are cases where the stepmother fills a vacuum and others in which she merely fools herself into thinking that there's a large space to fill.

If the natural mother is doing her job as mother, the stepmother's role is easier and infinitely less demanding. This stepmother would be foolish as well as presumptuous to attempt mothering. Where, however, the natural mother is and has been remiss as mother, or where she's out of the picture, a stepmother is called upon for more. The extent of that "more" is the question.

The stepmother with children in her home has obvious specific chores. Some experts feel that the operational level is the limit of her undertaking: she makes the children wash their hands, go to school, say thank you. She manages the household, sets up some guidelines, is a friendly adult, and stops.

Most stepmothers with full custody, however, feel an obligation to help a stepchild grow in an appropriate way. This is more feasible if a stepmother gets the children when they are young and malleable. If they are older, she has at least two strikes against her. As one stepmother put it, "I was the wrong person, and besides I came too late."

Many a stepmother has infinite difficulty raising children she didn't start. That stepmother needs to forgive herself—and the stepchildren. Ease off. Do what she can. She cannot do the impossible. Neither can the stepchildren. A biological mother isn't successful all the time—why on God's earth should a stepmother expect herself to be?

A great deal of the secret, in both full- and part-time step, lies in allowing the child to set the pace of the relationship. When it becomes too much for the child, the child will pull back. If the stepmother can wait, the child will return.

The role of the part-time stepmother is not as demanding as that of the full-time stepmother. It is more complicated and possibly less rewarding. There is more interference. The situation is kept agitated by the simple shifting of the children back and forth between homes. The antipathy that a child frequently drags between homes has to be slowly unloaded each time; each time there is a gradual reorientation process.

Depending on whether the stepmother is a once-a-month, once-a-week, or all-summer variety, her role varies. In each instance the experts (again!) suggest that she lay off. She can be teacher, friend, confidante, anything but mother.

LIMITS AND RESPONSIBILITIES

"It sounds easy," says Ruth. "Anything but mother! But I, for one, had trouble understanding the requirements and limits of my role. I could take the limits without the responsibilities, or the responsibilities without the limits. But both together?

"In the first place, I never had a stepmother to teach me how to be a stepmother. I only had a mother who taught me how to mother. If she was my friend, teacher, confidante, she was that within the person of Mother. And I am sure, looking at it retrospectively, that I believed I was just that—a part-time mother —just like my mom, only part time.

"The requirements. Whatever I was, one thing I surely was —a cook. In my capacity as part-time stepmother I have done an awful lot of cooking. Going to the grocery store, filling up the carts (two, sometimes), and dragging in the bags. Sometimes the boys would go with me and help me, but they liked to buy masses of junk. Somehow they never got fat.

"I remember somebody once asking me to do something.

" 'I can't!'

" 'Why not?'

" 'Because I cook twenty-four meals a day,' I shouted. I had counted it up: three meals a day for two adults, four children, and two friends who were around for the children.

"I mean, somebody had to feed them—that's the 'operational level' the experts allow the stepmother. But the operational level is no small matter. Clothes have to be bought (sometimes) and washed (always). Name tapes may have to be sewn on. And what about the kitchen floor again? Then arguments have to be settled. Dentists and doctors and always the orthodontist. Schools to visit. Crises to pray over. Children to talk to.

"Well, that's where I got confused. The limits. It sure looked like mothering to me. Until I got caught up short, again and again. I went too far. I also expected too much.

"After the first long summer when I had tried so hard, the boys sent their letters to their father's office. What about me? Wasn't I part of the family?

"Or, before we'd go on a special vacation, the oldest boy would in one way or another bring up his mother. He'd say, 'I wish Mom were going with us.' Or 'Ruth, would you lend me money to buy a present for Mom when we're down there?'

"I should have said, 'You miss your mother. You wish she

were going too.' Instead, I said, 'If you want money to buy your mother a present, you'll have to get it from your father. Not from me,' and I raced from the room—to wonder ever since if he asked for the money and if he got it.

"That's my problem. Even knowing better, as I now do (at least, wouldn't you think so?), I find it hard to accept the limits. A stepmother is not, repeat, is not a mother. But she sure is something. The question is always how much or how little of that something is she?"

TAKING ON TOO MUCH

The stepmother who takes on too much for her own reasonable limits may find herself stewing in the morass of her own resentments, thereby doing nobody any good. In that state, she will be the one to treat even the smallest request as an imposition.

The "cruel" stepmother is often born out of the woman who has been afraid to work out the limits of her responsibilities. The stepmother must with her husband clearly draw the lines as to what is expected of her. The important issue is deciding what she can take before the scene takes *her* into that downward spiral of dumb-dumb martyrdom. It takes some years to "admit" their resentments and to ask for their needs. This happens in many relationships, but it happens more often in step.

We cannot tell you where to draw your lines. Needs and tolerances are individual. But when that used-and-abused feeling begins to take over, that's the time to start talking about a restructuring of time and priorities.

If that doesn't happen—which is the case all too often in step—resentments get stored and savored, ferment, and finally explode.

Having had enough one stepmother told us: "Ken's daughters make me so unhappy that I can't see them any more. Ken can have them over any time he wants—when I'm not there. He can do whatever he wants with them, as long as I don't have to go with them."

Such can be the end result should the stepmother fail to make some early accommodation with her husband. It can get to the point where a stepmother is willing to risk her husband's relationship with his children and/or her marriage in order not to have to deal with the children.

Barbara drew no limits until she was emotionally and spiritually exhausted. She went into the marriage as Joan of Arc. We hope she doesn't leave as Marie Antoinette. She says:

"I had Joe's three children every other weekend and every summer for three years before I realized I couldn't take it. Then I continued to have them for three more years before I got the courage to say I didn't want to have them any more. Now I'm so bitter over all the things I hated and had to do that I don't think I can ever get over it.

"The greatest mistake I ever made was trying to be the supermother. I did it for Joe because I loved him so much. He kept encouraging me in this direction, saying I was a wonderful mother. I think he subconsciously was trying to provide them with something so warm they'd be unhappy when they returned to their own mother. And I also thought, Poor children, they have such a terrible mother. What I didn't think about was that they did have a mother, whatever she was like, and they would have to go back to her at the end of the summer.

"It was a gradual process by which I began to admit that ours wasn't a perfect family. For so long I couldn't let myself see that everything wasn't just fine, that I didn't have to be supermother. I did and did and did all the things I hated. I had no time for myself and not much for my children.

"At some point I noticed that the only times Joe did anything with my children was when his own were around.

"One day I said to myself, Do everything everybody else wants. Smile, make love, play games, cook, clean, launder, and sew on name tags. Suddenly I was overwhelmingly tired and resentful. I took my two children and went away for a week. We had a wonderful time just being alone and laughing and walking and having picnics. It was so good to be with them and not to feel guilty for enjoying them and giving them my attention. I realized how hard it has been in this marriage to spend time with my own children.

"When we came home again I admitted my resentments. I told Joe I didn't want to see his children every other weekend.

"It took me years to move from trying so hard to indifference, to anger. If I could do it over, I'd fight back sooner instead of waiting until it's too late to remove the resentments for everything we've done and everything we've lost. I'd ask more of Joe for my own children, and I'd give less of myself to his children. Then maybe the two of us could have had more time together."

Barbara's story is revealing in many ways. Perhaps the most important thing it reveals is the amount of anguish a stepmother might save if she remembered to view herself primarily as her husband's wife and not as his children's stepmother. A stepmother's first responsibility is to herself and her husband and their marriage. The rest comes after that.

4

The Stepmother's Wants

"THE STEPMOTHER'S WANTS"—the phrase itself may startle the stepfamily and even the stepmother herself. The children's needs, perhaps the husband's needs, seem to be overriding. We have found that this doesn't work. The stepmother whose own needs aren't met will not be a very good stepmother. Certainly she won't be a happy one.

What are her needs? Her desire for recognition seems to be a major one; the lack of it one of her deepest dissatisfactions. Acknowledgment and appreciation are often scarce commodities for the stepmother.

RECOGNITION FROM THE MOTHER

The same mother who will thank someone who takes one of her children for an afternoon will say nothing to the stepmother who takes all of her children for months. It's a point of contention. A stepmother wants from her husband's former wife, her stepchildren's mother, some admission in some form that she is doing something when the children are with her. She rarely gets it. Most mothers aren't about to admit—to themselves, much less to the stepmother—that stepmothering is what's going on in the other household.

Marilyn took her three new stepchildren to the mountains for a month. During the week, and on weekends when her husband was there, Marilyn pulled out all the stops to amuse the children, to be somebody they enjoyed being with. There was a novelty to the task, and she threw herself into it.

When she returned the children, nobody said thank you—not the father, the children, or their mother. The mother, an old friend of Marilyn's, offered not a single appreciative word. "Had she said thank you, even on the falsest level," Marilyn said, "it would have made a difference. It would have opened the door for a relationship. Her refusal to say anything set up a conflict that carried over—the whole trend of the relationship was set." Marilyn never again offered to take the children on a trip.

EMOTIONAL SUPPORT FROM THE HUSBAND

Most important to the stepmother is the clear, unequivocal support of her husband. He may, unfortunately, fail to realize that his wife's success as a stepmother relates directly to his ability to communicate emotional support. In almost every instance where we have found a gratified stepmother, we have also found a husband who understands, validates, and is simply there for his wife as stepmother. Again and again stepmothers have expressed to us their conviction that, through all their difficulties, the one thing that kept them going was their husbands' appreciation.

"I could never have made it with those kids if Sam hadn't backed me," one stepmother told us. "His teenagers were so difficult for me to handle that our marriage simply would not have survived had he not stood by me all the way. He not only made the punishments stick—when he saw I'd had a rough day, he'd say, 'Honey, I know it's hard on you. Let's get out some TV dinners for the kids, and you and I go out for dinner.' "

Often a stepmother feels manipulated into being a caretaker of other people's children, a babysitter for life. She suspects that the work she does profits the biological mother, possibly the father and children, but never herself. From the outside world, from the children, even from the father, the mother gets the credit for the child regardless of what the stepmother does. Sensing this, stepmothers talk of feeling used and used and used.

APPRECIATION FROM THE STEPCHILDREN

Almost to be expected—especially at the beginning—is the children's denial of her efforts. She cooks all afternoon, only to have a child say, "Mom's lasagne is better."

Even an oblique reward can encourage her to keep going. If children realized how easy it can be to alter the direction of a stepmother's behavior, the wicked stepmother might become an extinct species.

"There have been times when I have wondered, truly wondered," says Ruth. "Times when I have said good morning and gotten silence in return, times when I have spoken and gotten a sullen quietness for response. Still, whenever I get discouraged and maybe begin to resent or give up a little, it seems that one of my stepchildren will do something to encourage me, and I'm off and running again.

"A thousand ways they have rewarded me. Telephone calls, a hug returned, dishes washed, long talks into the night, laughter instead of criticism for a mistake of mine—and most of all, the cessation of hostilities and a growing honesty and kindness every year. It makes it all worth while."

Perhaps a rare stepmother can look to herself for the support she needs so badly. We doubt it. What comes from the outside feeds the inside. Sometimes it seems as though there's a conspiracy against the stepmother's self-esteem. She can feel almost as if she's being erased.

One family therapist told us of stepmothers who came to him for help feeling not only angry but humiliated. He had to work with them until they honestly felt that their concerns were legitimate.

The difficulty, of course, lies in the situation. The self-esteem of a stepmother whose primary activity is the family rests on her family's view of her. Yet the family mechanisms in step are working against her. In the natural family, the process of idealization boosts the image of the biological mother. The stepmother's image can't possibly equal that of the natural mother. Natural mothers *are* encouraged in their efforts—their children, anyway, think they're something. "That's my mom!" Not so with the stepmother.

MOM'S IS BETTER

One stepmother solved a my-mom's-is-better problem unexpectedly. Her stepson praised and praised his mom's chili; Stepmom set version after version before the child, who always managed to convey that, whatever the recipe, the result just wasn't as good as Mom's. The child's craving for "good" chili continued; the stepmother's enthusiasm for the cooking did not. One day she just gave up and bought chili in the can. The result? "Hey! This is just like Mom's! You finally made it!"

The next time one of her stepchildren threw a Mom's-xyz-is-better at her, the stepmother smiled and went with it. "I'm sure it is," she said. "How does she do it? Do you think you could find out for me?"

The problem, of course, goes beyond the Mom's-is-better syndrome. Not only is the stepmother not idealized, she may find herself on the receiving end of the anger for whatever the natural mother did or didn't do. On top of that, the children without being aware of it may feel they have to punish her for taking their mother's place. None of it bodes well for Stepmother's ego, and any family member with a damaged ego can become dangerous to the rest of the family.

WANTING TO COME FIRST

A stepmother wants to come first with her husband. If she feels that her husband's chief loyalty is to his children, she may do anything to come first with him—including trying to turn him against his children.

A friend of ours openly admits to hating her stepchildren. No, she didn't hate them from the beginning. It just grew, she says. What did they do? Well, just the usual things. Hostility, resentment, treating her like a servant, vying for their father's attentions and often winning over her. Of course, no matter what she did, their mother did it better. Plus they weren't very smart and had nothing in common with her—except, of course, her husband, their father.

As our cruel-stepmother friend tells it, things went from bad to worse to godawful. She threatened to leave. The scene with the children was excruciating. It's either-or! Me or the children! She and her husband fought. She left. They made up, and his children didn't come around much any more. When he saw them, it was by himself, outside of their home.

And she was first at last. Or was she?

Some stepmothers try to come first not only with their husbands but with their stepchildren as well—they believe they have earned the slot and try like crazy to achieve it. But a stepmother isn't at all likely to get the preponderant loyalty. And even if the children feel strong affection for her they are not likely to express it.

Feeling both secondary and closed out, a stepmother can become very angry indeed. Anything can happen, and whatever does happen can't help affecting the marriage.

"What I didn't realize," one stepmother told us, "was that I could never be a family with my husband and his children. Something was always working against it. By the time their exclusions stopped, mine began. I think he thought that by marrying me he'd have his old family back again with a new twist, a better wife and mother. It just didn't work out.

"I would love to have us be the primary unit—then anything else could come and go and we could weather it. The way it is now, our love is truncated. I'm fighting for a position I can never have, and I'm tired of crashing against locked gates."

A CHILD OF OUR OWN

A stepmother may want, very badly, her own child in the new marriage—a child conceived and naturally shared between her and her husband, a child with whom she will come first.

Sally wants a baby. Somehow she and Ernie never discussed this before marriage. After marriage she discovered that he didn't want any more children. It was all he could do to pay child support, doctor bills, tuition, and so forth for his four children. He wanted to share his love for them with Sally.

"They're our children, Sally. Aren't they enough for you?"

"Frankly, no. It's not the same, Ernie."

To us she said, "They're not my kind of kids. I couldn't conceivably have had them or raised them."

Right now, Ernie swings back and forth. He brings his own children to the small apartment every weekend, but he enjoys their weekly quietness together. Sally is not about to give up her dream: someday she will have a baby of her own.

Grace is a stepmother who had the same dream. Her husband had three children; she had one. He wanted no more. "Let's enjoy this part of our lives," he said. "The kids are finally growing up."

"Please, please, please."

"No, no, no."

Then, one night when they were walking down the street, he gave in. Grace stood there in the middle of the sidewalk, warmed and gratified, crying with happiness. Now she felt she really was his wife.

Months passed into years, and she still wasn't pregnant. To Grace, it hardly matters any more. He loves her enough to give her his baby: a baby isn't any longer essential to her happiness.

The problem for the stepmother lies in the fact that her husband did have children with another woman. The mere existence of those children can conflict with her own maternal instincts. Priorities are distorted, loyalties tangled. A marriage without children between the husband and wife can feel somehow less than a marriage. That it can be something equally as good is an idea many women find hard to accept.

THE OTHER WOMAN IN HIS LIFE

Somebody once said, "There are too many people in a second marriage." That's for certain.

The former wife seems to be everywhere in the new step marriage: she's in the language and traditions of the family, in the children's memories and personalities. Should she be far away, the past persists in the new marriage. Should she have died, the memories are preserved if not enshrined. More or less, one way or the other, she's there.

Question: How does the stepmother handle the prior wife?

Answer: As little as possible.

Would that it were so easy. It isn't. Bygones are not bygones, nor can they be in step. For, while the former couple have obtained a legal divorce, they cannot get a parental divorce. They continue together in a mother-father relationship to their mutual children.

Until the children are out on their own, the two must keep in touch and make arrangements. There is an indissoluble bond between them—whatever their feelings for each other—that often excludes the second wife. A bitter, rankling fact.

We have seen many a stepmother fall into competition with the former wife, especially if the husband is still fond of her. She may strive to prove herself superior in any or all ways—as wife, mother, cook, housekeeper, conversationalist, career woman. She wants to be better dressed, prettier, more honest: she wants to be more of whatever the other woman is or isn't. And, of course, she hopes that her husband and children will take note.

The husband may; the children usually won't. That would be disloyal to Mom. Should the stepmother continue to make a point of her "superiority" and try to force concessions, she may propel them into more hostility toward her and loyalty toward their own mother. She may well be setting herself up to get the opposite of what she wants.

Should her husband intensely dislike his former wife, the stepmother may feel no need to compete—other than to prove that she's not like *her!* And, if the former wife remarries, she's likely to create fewer difficulties for the stepmother.

However, many an ex-wife is still at war with her ex-husband. The husband can suffer spiteful revenge at her hands; the new wife is left to deal with the moods. The former wife may even work at creating levels of guilt in him so that he can never be free.

"You wouldn't believe how *she* manipulates us all by her inability to cope," one stepmother says. "She has an instinct for bringing calamity down on her head, and by indirection everybody else's head as well, including mine. If it isn't physical illness, it's mental illness. If it isn't illness, it's money troubles. And, when it's not money, it's her own life that seems to get in the way of her raising her own children. Again and again, she denies them in answering her own needs. But the funny thing is, they never blame her."

The prior and current families both exist. They may be enemies out there in the fields of step. And the stepmother seems to be standing right in the middle of that open field with little armor other than her wits and awareness.

One thing she can do is not retaliate in kind. If she goes along accepting the mother and prior wife, the others won't feel the need to defend her. Should the prior wife be dead, the next wife is likely to hear nothing but the wonders of this woman. She should understand, reduce it all at least by half, join the group—even repeat some of the good things she's heard. By accepting instead of fighting against the former wife, alive or dead, the stepmother can create for herself a far more comfortable world.

Many a wife in step has complained that her husband sometimes refers to his ex-spouse as his wife. She overhears him at a party, saying, "My wife is taking me to court next month to up her child support." *She* is not! Or "When my wife and I camped out in Yellowstone . . ." *She*'s never been to Yellowstone!

Well, sometimes one mixes up the names of one's children. Why not wives? One of the great lubricants of life is humor. So step-second-wife walked up to her husband telling a chum at a cocktail party about marvelous Yellowstone, and she continued the tale. Told fabulous fabrications. Her husband grew embarrassed and started to say, "Hey!" He stopped as she giggled at him. He noted the nomenclatures of his wives a little better after that.

Sometimes a stepmother is able to relax and enjoy a friendship with her husband's former wife. Since people have a tendency to marry the same type of person over again, a man's wives are likely to have some resemblance whether in character, personality, or appearance. Similarities can create an attraction between the two women—if each respects and accepts the functions of the other.

While the husband's ex-wife sometimes belongs to the past, the husband's daughters decidedly belong to the present. As we interviewed stepmothers of stepdaughters, we noticed that the stories had begun to sound painfully alike. Many of the women were extremely attractive and had never before given much thought to the female competition.

Now these women were unsteadied by the behavior of a stepdaughter. Her age didn't necessarily matter: she could be a very young girl or a grown woman. What did matter was that these wives were bested, many of them for the first time in their lives.

One friend wrote us a touching letter just after her baby daughter had been born. She'd had natural childbirth and her husband had been with her. They were brought very close.

Three days later his twenty-two-year-old married daughter arrived at the hospital. She dropped some flowers on a table, saying, "These are for you." That was the extent of her reference to the birth of the baby. She barely left her father's side during her entire visit, never giving the couple a moment alone. She pursued her game of oneupsmanship at every opportunity. Finally, her stepmother gave up the struggle and each evening sent father and daughter out for dinner. Why, she asked, should she have to submit herself and her baby to all this resentment?

One full-time stepmother told us that her fourteen-year-old stepdaughter would sit on her father's lap and kiss him. When they got into the car to go someplace, she would jump in right beside him. If there was a decision to be made about where they were going, they went where the stepdaughter wanted to go. If she didn't want to go somewhere, they wouldn't go.

"At times," she said, "I felt she was as seductive as a full-grown woman, trying to take her father away from me. She resented the fact that we were sleeping in the same bed and that she couldn't come into the bedroom whenever she liked. We developed a terrible sexual problem from lack of time and privacy. It got to the point that I packed my bags, but I had no place to go."

Marriage counselor Dr. Esther Oshiver Fisher believes that what has to happen in a second marriage is what should have happened in the first marriage. "A unity develops between the couple. It is a closed-bedroom affair, literally and metaphorically. The door is closed to the relationship: they are the unit. When either walks out, they walk out to children or ex-spouses, but they walk out as part of that unit."

We asked Dr. Tec what a stepmother who feels utterly undermined by a stepdaughter should do.

"Lay off."

"Lay off whom?"

"The idea that she will be a mother—such a wonderful mother that the daughter will not be a force between them."

"No," we said, "she's not trying to be a mother. She's trying to be a wife. And she feels that the daughter comes between her and her husband."

"Naturally. The daughter has to. This should have been considered before they got married. You don't take it seriously, but it's inevitable. Any woman who marries a man with a daughter will have to remember that. If she doesn't, she's blind or naïve."

"Well, they're mostly naïve. We all are when we remarry."

"Most people idealize future relationships—whether it's marriage, boyfriends and girlfriends, or business."

"Well, what about the father and husband? What could he do?"

"He can do a lot, because he can have time for his daughter and time for his wife. He can realize that what his daughter is doing can be destructive if he falls prey to it. He has to be the moderating factor. *She* has to take it lightly, and *he* has to deal with it."

Jeannette's solution:

"One Labor Day weekend, one of the girls was with us. I felt as if Bob had two wives, and there was a lot of bickering going on among the three of us. I tabulated the whole situation in this IBM

360 computer I carry around in my head. [That, says Ruth, is an idealized concept of Jeannette's head.] Space . . . what our scene needs is space for the father and daughter to be alone. Neither will come straight out and ask for it. So Mrs. Machiavelli Manipulata will arrange.

"Shopping to be done? 'Hey, husband and stepdaughter, would you do that?'

"Trip home? 'Bob, we have two cars. How about you driving home with Jennifer. Give you a chance to talk in private—you haven't seen each other in a while.'

"I gave them the space they needed that they couldn't ask for. And our feelings toward one another were better all the way around."

Give back the turf to your stepdaughters whenever you can. You have to realize that you have taken their territory. It's rightfully yours, and it's rightfully theirs. It's all hard to talk about and even harder to share back. But by stepping back and allowing space alone with the father, you find there's more room for you. That's one of the tricky rewards in step.

HOW TO BECOME THE CRUEL STEPMOTHER

There is a pattern in the evolution of resentment and retaliation. In that pattern grow the seeds of birth for the cruel stepmother. The source of cruelty is the situation and not the person. How not to become the cruel stepmother is hard. How to become the cruel stepmother is easy.

Simply put, here's how it can work. The stepmother offers interest and attention to the child. The stepchild responds with coldness, indifference. The stepmother tries, keeps trying for a period, then finally withdraws. She takes a fixed position—a distant one. The stepchild finds his original negative assumption confirmed ("I always knew she was mean"). The child may attempt to break up the marriage. The stepmother retaliates. Through all kinds of actions, or inactions, a child may force choices to be made by his father. If the father sides with the child over the stepmother, the family is in trouble. The stepmother tries to win the father over to her side. At any rate, she wants to have the stepchild around less and less. Here she usually succeeds. Sooner or later, everybody gets into the act, and the scene is set for a traditional wicked-stepmother play—sticky, mean, and heartbreaking.

There are also surprises that jar the stepmother into withdrawal. Just as the scene has begun to evolve into something warm and friendly, a stepchild may do something that makes her feel all her efforts and hard-won gains amount to very little after all. Thus, years back, Ruth wrote her first stepmother poem:

Okay then, go ahead and say it.
I am cruel. As you say I am.
Stepmother with a twisted heart.
Old virgin in a dry land,
Wet nurse to a vacant world.

Whatever way you look at it,
You can't recycle other people's children.
You can't live in a family bolted together
Like an emotional lean-to.
Flimsy construction—weeds shoving out of every crack,
And the absentee landlord demanding all the rent.

I am rattling dirty dishes
In someone else's dream,
doing up the laundry
In someone else's life.
Couldn't I have had something
Not quite so second hand?
Something clean and shiny,
And all my very own?

Look here, I say.
You handed me the empty pages
Of a book I never wrote.
You colored all the edges of my words,

took away my punctuation,
Left me hovering on a pause . . .
Then you asked me for a poem.

Okay, then, go ahead and say it.
I am cruel. As you say I am.
But who, in God's name, tell me,
Loves those—who don't love them?

BREAKING THE CYCLE

The problem becomes one of breaking the cycle.

One way is to withdraw from too heavy a concentration on the scene. Get out. Get away. Play, do volunteer work, do anything, but do it. Many therapists recommend that a stepmother work, if only part time. Many a stepmother has told us that she would never have made it if she hadn't worked.

One woman we know got married, and a year later she got three boys. Her domestic role increased threefold, and the amount of loving and attention she received seemed to be diminished by the same amount. (Generally, if there's one thing stepchildren easily accept, it is that the servile tasks will be taken care of by the stepmother.) Her solution? She went out and got herself a job. She works three days a week, and now all of the family members divide up the work.

Another way to break the cycle is to become absorbed in the adventure of making it work. A stepmother who pulls back and assesses the situation is better able to see what's going on. If she can understand the dynamics of step, she may be more inclined to forgive and to work some changes.

In second marriages, there is a greater reluctance to allow the expression of any negative feelings. Having experienced one failure, a couple is fearful of another. The result is the bottling-up of discontents. Stepchildren do the same thing. By holding the feelings in instead of letting them out and later talking about them, a family can actually bring to pass whatever misfortunes they were trying to avoid. Resentments become ossified, the atmosphere is unfriendly, nobody really knows what's eating the others.

What almost has to happen at this point is a confrontation. Jeannette had one early in her marriage. Ruth waited for years:

"One evening I was alone in the Bahamas with the four kids. Bill had just gone back to New York to work, and we were to be there together for another week. Outside our house on a lonely white beach, the surf was crashing. We should have been happy. We weren't.

"It had been a long summer. One of my stepsons had continually been going after my son. Another had been going after me. The situation had become so tortured that I didn't care any longer. I just let go. I let them have it. The boys let go. They let me have it. We talked. We cried. Each one of us was surprised that the others had legitimate gripes. And there were things that each of us could do about them. When we finished, there was enormous relief and euphoria.

"The next day some children who visited us went home and told their mother, 'It's so much fun at the Roosevelts'. They laugh all the time.' Believe me, we weren't laughing the day before.

"That evening was a turning point in my relationship with my stepsons. There was a new easiness. We knew what was going on, and we were able to work toward compromise."

Another way to break the cycle is to seek professional counseling. Many troubled step marriages work through to an operational success by getting some form of family therapy. Sometimes it takes only a few sessions.

The time has come to stop feeling shame or failure for step difficulties. They're endemic to the situation, and they *can* be helped.

RACHEL

Rachel, the stepmother in the preceding chapter to whom "love happened" during a summer visit, found that she could see no way out of the difficulties once her husband gained custody of this son they both loved.

Rachel is a full-time copywriter and for three years now she has been a full-time stepmother as well. It took her over a year to feel good about having her stepson. To her, the time seemed an eternity. We consider one year a very short amount of time to come from and go to where she now is in step.

We asked her to complete this sentence: "If I had only known then what I know now . . ."

"I know what it would be," she said in her southern accent. "It would certainly have to be: If I had only known, *this too shall pass.*

"At first we had Alan only for the summers. Then we were to keep him for a few months during the school year. And finally, at the age of eleven, he came to live with us completely.

"It's hard to believe today that two years ago at this very time I was practically suicidal over that child. So was my husband. He worried over his son, and he worried over what the whole thing was doing to me. We felt our marriage under fire from Alan. His problems unsteadied and shook everything in our world. Our life was *consumed* with discussing him and reeling under the onslaught of his problems. All of our energies were spent on Alan!

"Until he came to us, Alan had moved from apartment to apartment, school to school. He'd never had a chance to sustain relationships. Living with us, he easily made friends—and then proceeded, seemingly helplessly, to lose friend after friend. The quality of the boys he chose as friends went progressively down. He spent little time with them anyway, because he was leaning so heavily on us for companionship and solace in his helpless, terribly disturbing situation.

"Finally things got so bad that one after the other of us became really ill. For the first time in months, bedridden and running a high temperature, my husband and I were alone. (We were, thank heavens, contagious.) We probably allowed ourselves to become ill just to be together.

"We decided that Alan needed professional help. Perhaps the troubles would have passed without it. We'll never know.

We do know that a year later, at twelve, Alan was a different child."

A friend of the family described Alan to us "before" and "after." When she first met him, she felt he was a "really rotten kid," loaded with repressed anger, and probably dangerous. He had chains wrapped around his wrists and reminded her of a handsome young hell's angel.

The first night she visited the house, she remembers, he did everything conceivable to provoke his father into paying even more attention to him. It ended up with his father springing out of his chair, shoving Alan—hard—and sending him flying. As Alan was lying there on the floor, his father came and stood over him, saying, "I don't ever want you to do that again." She remembers Alan looking pleased as he lay there. He had been fighting for affection and discipline, asking, "Is there anybody out there who cares enough to stop me?"

The friend didn't see him again for a year and a half. When she did, she was amazed. Alan had turned from a hostile, miserably unhappy boy into a polite, talkative twelve-year-old.

"He asked about my work and made mature comments. I mean, one could actually have a conversation with this kid. I couldn't believe it—the change. The year before he was muscling around trying to find his place. Now he'd found it. He acted easy and a part of the family."

Rachel says, "This unpopular child, who hung heavily on our necks, is now so busy with his friends and activities that it is we who have to say, 'Hey, when are you going to be home for an evening? We *miss* you!'

"That year seems like a nightmare, a horrible dream that I never really had. Had I only believed *this too shall pass!* It did. Problems still arise, of course—that's life—but with the relationships basically working, we can all deal with them as they come."

Here we see the happy dénouement of a step story which could have ended up as a total tragedy or, at least, an ongoing difficult situation. It didn't. The stepfamily worked its way out of its difficulties and ended up stronger, as a unit and individually, for the experience.

There are a number of factors at work in this particular family which combined to produce a stepmother who's happy to be one.

First, when the crisis became severe, she and her husband sought professional help. They *might* have made it without help, but action was indicated, and they took it.

Also, once Alan came to live with them full time, they were able to consolidate their gains and work on building a family without the interference of the mother. The husband and wife were not in conflict over her—she was a factor in their lives to be dealt with, not a threat that came between them.

This stepmother is able to talk of the mother with a tone of amusement in her voice. She accepts her as Alan's mother, however nomadic has been her life style. "She would change jobs, lovers—and Alan's schools—on an average of once a year. Yet she definitely gave Alan the vital ingredient of love, so important during his formative years, and I'm grateful to her for that essential base."

Alan has learned to accept both mother and stepmother. Because of his former difficulties, he understands the importance of the "new" woman who filled his life on a day-to-day basis. His stepmother consciously tries not to replace the mother, and respects the love Alan feels for her. He loves them both.

Important also is the fact that Rachel went to work every day. And she was highly respected at her job—every day she had the opportunity to go out and get her self-esteem replenished. It was not eroded by the turmoil within the family. Of course, it was shaken at times—often she felt helpless. But she didn't sink into helplessness.

Rachel feels that the most crucial factor to her success as a stepmother has been the total support and involvement of her husband. During the difficult period, they continually talked the problems over together. He didn't try to pretend they didn't exist, that, for example, it was just a stage his son was going through. The father took on most of the disciplining. When Rachel disciplined, he thoroughly supported her. He understood her struggles, for he shared them with her. They were a team.

Okay, we hear you saying. Your situation is not at all the

same. Of course not. Neither is ours. Every step relationship is totally particular. Unique.

Not every problem can be cured, but it can be minimized. The most important thing, Stepmother, is to take care of yourself, to take responsibility for yourself. Without doing this, you can't take care of those around you. We know, Stepmother, in order to fulfill your role you've got to be a kind of psychological and philosophical athlete. You've got to be in shape and okay with yourself. So understand your limits, talk things out with your husband and the kids, try to take things lightly—laugh if you can, and go out and get professional help if you need it. Take care of you.

5

The Stepfather

THAT MORNING THEY lay together in bed, their bodies lazily linked, enjoying the peaceful aftermath of Saturday-morning lovemaking.

For once, the kids were gone. For once they had silence and privacy. For once, she wasn't jumping up to do something for her children. Even their fights had stopped for a while. God, why couldn't it always be this way?

Bruce's stepchildren had gone on one of their rare weekend jaunts with their father. Fishing this time. With a little luck, the three of them would miraculously disappear at sea. . . . No, his luck would never hold.

Funny, the way the jokes had started. They'd be sitting in a restaurant with the children restless and jerking the chairs around, and he'd say, "Hey, kids, why don't you go outside and play in the traffic?"

Or Bobby (it was Bobby he usually aimed at) would run in claiming to have found some quicksand.

"Come and see it."

"I'll come and look if you promise to walk in it," he'd say with a laugh.

Finally even Nancy began to laugh. She realized, of course, that he half meant the things he said, but the kids never took it seriously.

All during those first years, the thoughts would come unbidden. The children were late getting home: maybe they'd been killed in an accident. Just fleeting fantasies. He did care. He was involved. Maybe too involved. Particularly with Kim; he loved her as much as either of his own. Almost. Maybe even more.

It's just that there was no way out of the mess. Unless you gave up the woman you wanted. Nancy . . . He was probably addicted to her.

Needing her, loving her, he had married her. He'd realized that she came as a package. What he hadn't comprehended was the size of the package. He'd thought that the children would be no big problem once they were married—that the children would interfere less after he and Nancy were married. That he'd have her more.

Instead, the kids devoured their marital time. He'd come home from work and want to be with Nancy. The children would barge in endlessly, interrupting or just hanging around listening. He'd seen it go wrong in his last marriage, with the kids out of control and his ex dumping the day's frustrations on him the minute he walked in the door. He and Nancy had talked it over. They would have a special reunion time: it would be peaceful, recuperative, fun—and private.

True, he and Nancy had made it a policy to be generally available to both children for their needs. But they had allowed too much. The children seemed to have a high priority to interrupt and thwart adult needs.

Dinners these days were a circus, a classic study of American waste. After dinner Nancy would spend the evenings helping with homework, settling fights, whatever. By the time they'd get to bed and get anything going, one of the kids would as likely as not bang on the door with some "problem," and Nancy would always be there for them. What about themselves?

Even the marital fights seemed dominated by the subject of children. And they'd had some beauts. They didn't seem to fight about what they were doing to each other; over and over, they fought about the children, his and hers. They'd start out for a dinner and an evening alone and spend half the time in yet another argument about the kids. . . .

"Hey, Nancy, baby, don't go away. Stay with me. I just got lost in my thoughts for a while."

He grabbed her and pulled her back in bed.

"I thought your mind had taken a walk! What were you thinking about?"

"Believe me, you don't want to hear it. Listen, let me bring you breakfast in bed."

He kissed her lightly and bounded down to the kitchen. Coffee, orange juice, toast, an omelet. It was fun to rattle around the kitchen in the buff, knowing that neither Bobby nor Kim nor any of their friends would descend upon him. He loved to cook. Provided the dinners weren't *family* dinners.

His friend Slater was actually considering marrying a woman with three kids. He'd better warn him: "Man, take a good, hard look before you do anything. You see them now and then before you get married, but afterwards they surround you."

Carrying the tray, he kicked the door open with his foot. Looking at Nancy, at her white, white breasts and pale tumbling hair, he realized he'd do it all over again. Even knowing what he now knew. It was just that somebody else's children were an incredible intrusion on your life. . . .

THE INTRUSION

The intrusion of the children, stated one way or another, is a recurring theme when stepfathers talk. Almost all we interviewed had underestimated the size of the undertaking, the magnitude of the problems. Almost none had foreseen the extent to which their lives would be changed by children.

For some stepfathers, of course, the children were a welcome addition: "Kids keep you young. You know, you can get lonesome without them. They give you that aliveness that occupies your mind. But you've got to like kids. . . ."

Other stepfathers spoke of the diversion of their time, energy, and resources.

"I thought at first I might be sharing the house with another family. So many strangers in the house, it got on my nerves. You wouldn't mind taking on a family in a disaster, but if they never left . . . ?"

"The child became a major concern. Instead of living our

own lives, we were living a life that was concerned with her. Gone were the conversations on any *other* subject."

"I don't think she will ever know what we were trying to do for her regardless of the costs. A child is an entirely different contract from a wife. With a wife you have an exchange. With a child, particularly if it isn't your child, you don't. It's a complex idea. Somebody, a child, has a demand upon you; yet you have very little demand upon that somebody, that child."

The step marriage affects not only the stepfather's time, but also his possessions.

One stepfather comments on his sense of invasion. "It was a game of attrition, very distressing.

"My wife and stepdaughter moved in with a cat. The cat would run all over my antiques. I'd collected them for years. Her cat would claw the upholstery, run up the drapes, and so forth. The first great crisis was that the cat had to go. Although the child was unhappy, she accepted the idea that the cat didn't fit the scene.

"My office room became the child's room. She was disadvantaged in acquiring many things that weren't designed for her. In setting up the room, I gave her my desk and other things.

"The child was incorrigibly messy. There she was in my quiet and orderly study. The first thing she did was tape the freshly painted walls with pictures of horses and rock stars. The place where I had everything neatly filed became strewn with clothes, papers, tools, whatever. The place where I had had quiet and thoughtful conversation with my friends now became the sounding chamber for stereophonic horrors.

"I would reason with her to no avail. Her dirty hands would sweep across the white couches. Finally, I developed the idea that she could be herself in her room as long as she didn't spread her mess in the rest of the house.

"As I look at it now, it was a process of educating Stepfather. Some children are very neat. My stepchild was not. There were moments of great rage when I would scream. In most of my business life I never screamed.

"A friend of mine used to talk of building a special house for his stepchildren with a little gangway between the children's house and the couple's lavish house. I remember visiting him and watching as one of his stepchildren knocked over a glass of wine on an oriental rug. The mother did nothing. I could see his inner rage. It was a tremendous conflict for him. He didn't last very long. He dropped dead shortly after marrying. Well, that's the ultimate way out when you can't handle something."

ESTABLISHING AUTHORITY

The stepmother operates against omnipresent myths of cruelty. The stepfather operates against an absence of myth, an unspoken assumption that his role is to play no role.

Yet he does have a definite role to play. He is the male head of the household, just as his wife is the female head of the household. The difficulty lies in establishing the position.

Almost all stepfathers agree that head-of-the-household authority doesn't come automatically. Some say it has to be earned; others say it needs to be asserted. Either way, establishing the position is a delicate matter. If the stepfather moves too quickly, the mother and stepchildren may recoil. The same thing may happen if he tries too hard. Yet, if he is not forceful enough, he may be disregarded.

A stepfather can establish his authority, right from the start, by leading rather than by commanding. If he gives his opinion, if he says what he feels, he directs without bossing or using demeaning criticism. Eliminating the heavy commands, he can nonetheless set a tone and aura of leadership.

"Don't do that!" "Stop it!" "Do this!"—and he soon has insubordination or enemies on his hands. If he can balance negatives with positives, people in the family will be less likely to feel put down.

Many stepfathers of boys who have been living with their single mothers for a number of years complain of what they call sissy behavior. It's hard. The child has had no male in-house model to pattern after. The rewards for his behavior are given by a woman who naturally tends to favor behavior closer to her own. Ergo, you may get a boy who shies away from rough play, or uses female tactics to get out of a rough situation. He simply has not had as much opportunity to learn male behavior at home.

There is also a tendency in a single-parent household to vest the boy as he gets older with masculine duties and chores. This sets up a natural competitive situation between the boy and the new man of the house.

Living together, a mother and a son may have developed a close relationship. The entrance of the stepfather, and the intensity of the new marital relationship, can be a threat to the son. The two males, the adult and child, may find themselves involved in an intense competition for the same woman.

Bruce traced his fingertips gently down Nancy's arms and felt her stiffening.

"What's the matter?"

"You have no sense of Bobby's feelings—whatsoever. You just lash out and ride all over him. Then you wonder why he lacks self-confidence."

Bobby must have gone bitching to her again. He'd come down to breakfast to find out that Bobby had done neither his last night's chores nor his homework. There he was—in a course he was flunking—racing to slop up a last-minute paper for school.

The boy needed some firming up in order to amount to anything. The concept that boys should be treated differently from girls was not something Nancy could deal with. He'd been disgusted with the kid that morning. He'd probably gone overboard in attempting to straighten him out, but one thing had led to the next. When the kid had told him to shut up, he'd cuffed him one.

Ever since they'd been married, he'd tried to erect a structure within which the child could operate. It was impossible, because Nancy would always disagree with one of the parameters. All he could do was poke at particulars and hope for improvement in some area.

Tightening his fingers around her wrist, he said, "Look, Nancy, do you want Bobby to continue to act like a baby for whom everything is done?"

"Do you think he's going to grow up by your screaming at him?"

"Listen to me carefully," Bruce said in a low voice. "You married me, a certain kind of man with a certain kind of goals and virtues. You asked me to help you raise the children. It's worked with Kim. It hasn't worked with Bobby. But, as long as I'm the man in this house, I'm going to have to do it the only way I know how. I've got too many years in that boy to let him sink further into his jellyfish mire. You've got to trust me."

"Trust you!" She pulled her hand away and launched another of her tirades.

He knew that Bobby had made up another three-ton story. He also knew that he'd back off from disciplining for a while. . . .

THE DELICATE BALANCE OF DISCIPLINE

Discipline and love go hand in hand. Too much love without the direction of discipline, or too much discipline without the support of love, can create serious deficiencies in the child and child-parent relationship.

Discipline and love need to be balanced, in or out of step. But in step the love is often hard to feel. The blood and the history are missing. Even where the objectives are the same, a biological father may remember things that soften the need to discipline. A stepfather has fewer brakes on his discipline.

The harshness of the discipline may be exacerbated by the resentments inherent in step situations. The child may test; the adult may prove. As the stepfather is neither sage nor saint, he may be pushed beyond his limits and allow his anger to be fueled by the hostility and testing of the child.

That sets the stage for the mother to lunge like a tigress to the defense of her cubs: "How dare you treat him like that!" Through one means or another she may build her biological fences, beyond which the stepfather is not welcome.

No fool, he withdraws. The pattern, unfortunately, is often classic. The stepfather disciplines the child. The child goes to the mother. The mother supports the child. She becomes angry and takes it out on the stepfather, sexually or in some other way.

At this point she effectively discourages the stepfather from interacting with her children. She stops the transactions between stepchild and stepfather. Then she complains that the stepfather has withdrawn. In the meantime, the behavior of the child that upsets the stepfather gets worse. His relationship with the child shrinks.

Mother is in the middle. All transactions go through her, leaving stepfather and child with a translated relationship.

Half the burden to work the problem out with his wife is on the stepfather. Half the burden is on the mother as well. What can she do?

"She can trust her husband," says marriage counselor Dr. Oshiver Fisher.

"But what if she feels he doesn't have the right instincts and restraints with her children?"

"She trusted him with her life. Why not trust him with her children as well?"

"If it doesn't work?"

"Then it's time for a meaningful discussion in which both husband and wife communicate their feelings in a constructive and benign manner," Dr. Fisher said.

Some stepparents report that they find it easier to discipline each other's children. Many mothers expressed gratitude for the stepfather's guidance and discipline. One stepfather put it this way: "It's a beautiful thing when the mother says, 'This is my husband, your stepfather. Together we are bringing you up.' "

DOING FOR OTHERS' CHILDREN

Head of his household, the stepfather may be burdened by the sad fact that his own children are not part of his household. They may not be getting the kind of fathering he would have given them if . . .

Bruce's ex-wife had called him at work that morning, worried about their oldest daughter, Margie. It seemed last night she had come home late, wouldn't say where she'd been, and wouldn't speak to her mother in the morning.

"Bruce, I just can't control her any more. The girls need a father—especially now that they're teenagers. It's your turn, damnit. Can't you at least take them for the summer?"

By the time he had hung up, a tightness had filled up his chest. Love. Guilt. Worry. Ambivalence. Christ! Other children were jamming up his life. Why couldn't his own be part of it?

Sometimes he'd wake up at night, aching with feelings for his daughters. God damn it! He loved them and they loved him. The love was *reciprocal.* He wondered at his involvement with another man's children while his own were getting lost out there for the want of a little fatherly love and discipline.

Nancy would never go for the whole summer routine. But he had to take the girls! Margie wouldn't pull that crap with him. He'd straighten her out in no time. God, it was scary the way Tory was becoming a mirror of her mother, the same gestures, same weak voice. He had to get them out of there.

He'd have a talk with Nancy. Maybe he'd better start with something small like Tory's birthday party. Then he'd say, "Nancy, love, you've got to help me. You're great with girls, and, well, look what you've done with Kim, and my girls—" What the hell! Did he have to plan out a script begging his wife for the privilege of including his own daughters in the scheme of things? Look what he did for Kim and Bobby! He'd give it to her straight. "Nancy, Babes, this is it. Take it or leave it."

Christ! What if she left it . . . ?

Nancy. The sweet thrust of her critical and laughing mind. Her body a road map to his love. Christ! Who were the others to puncture their love?

The stepfather finds himself fathering another's children while his own are elsewhere. A profound frustration, that—to do for the other's children what you are not able to do for your own. One may pity the stepmother, described in one dictionary definition as a bird that sits on another bird's eggs; but the stepmother, at least, is not usually separated from her own brood.

When his own children visit, the stepfather finds himself overcompensating, or at least being accused of going overboard. He sees them all too little, and he tries to build in a few hours what he has days or weeks to do with his stepchildren. He may be more concerned about doing things together than he is when the stepfamily is alone. To his wife and stepchildren his efforts look lopsided. The mother feels he is giving more time and attention and energy and even money to his own rather than to her and hers.

The discipline looks pretty unequal too. One of his kids may do something that calls for a strong hand. He would have administered it were he in the old family, living with the child. Now he hesitates. He's courting his kids. He doesn't want to lose them. His wife may feel that a legitimate punishment has to be meted out, while the stepchildren may think that *his* kids are getting away with murder.

The scene implies favoritism. The wife and stepchildren may even read it as a betrayal or rejection of themselves. He doesn't see the unevenness. If anything, he feels the basic imbalance is in favor of his new family.

THE IDEAL OF EQUAL LOVE

Yet many stepfathers will maintain that they love their stepchildren as much as their own. A family can hold so tightly to the ideal of equal love that any evidence to the contrary is taken as unkindness or even cruelty. It's a family convention that can amount to a painful fiction.

The truth is that most stepfathers in no way feel the same about children and stepchildren. Where the biological tie is missing, there is a difference in the quality and the depth of feeling. Not facing up to that difference creates problems. It throws a heavy burden of pretense on the family.

This sort of fathering stance is frequently thrust upon the stepfather by the mother. It goes "love me, love my child—I am your wife, she is your daughter—he is your son . . ."

Such a mother may be angry or disappointed with the natural father. Or she may be fearful that the father will attempt to take the children from her. Or perhaps the father has simply disappeared. Understandably, in such a situation, she wants to maintain the stepfather-as-father fiction.

We have an egocentric and flamboyant friend who is an autocratic father and stepfather. He insists that his stepson is his son. He even goes so far as to hint at his biological fathering of the child.

Perhaps our friend is, in this case, more than stepfather. We wouldn't know. We do know, however, that at the time the child was born he had a legal father whom he still sees and still loves. And that is the central fact.

Our friend demands that his stepson call him "Dad." He also demands that he use his surname. The child's father, of course, expects the child to use *his* last name.

When the little boy reached five he entered school. Here he could not use two surnames; he had to settle on one. He had a conflict of authorities as well as loyalties. Two roads crossed in his heart, and then they crossed in his life. He stood stuck, looking down the two ways.

At this point, a psychiatrist stepped in and helped him. She explained to him the dual fathering in his life. He had a father who helped him be born, and a father who was helping him to be raised. Since the name he was born with was his legal name, that was the name he should use in school.

The mother is behind this stepfather's attitude. She wants her husband to consider himself the boy's father. She won't, she says, have it any other way. She also wants the child's father out of the picture, and she can find authorities to support her position. He isn't, however, about to give up his son.

And so there are two fathers insistently fathering one small boy.

Yet we can see that our friend does not act toward his stepchild the way he does toward his own children. Nor does his stepchild behave toward him the way his own children do. Children know the difference. The verbal stance doesn't jibe with the covert feelings or the overt behavior.

To what extent a stepparent should be parent is one of the most important unsettled questions in step relationships. For the stepfather the only approximate definition of role we have belongs to the father role. Thus we think in terms of a stepfather as a father. It's contradictory, since the stepfather is also enjoined from taking the father's place.

WHAT IS STEPFATHERING?

At the same time, the stepfather is spurred on by the moral axiom that he is to do an adequate job of stepfathering. The question is, what is stepfathering?

For many stepchildren the father has to all intents and purposes dropped out of the picture. Even where the father remains in the picture, the primary male figure may well be the stepfather with whom they live.

The degree of necessary male parenting, of course, varies according to the needs of the child and the abilities of the parent.

In interviewing stepchildren we found many who longed for their stepfathers to take more active roles, do more things with them, show signs of caring about them. They wanted their stepfathers to be more like fathers, not less like them. And they wanted it poignantly.

One stepson told a judge, "He's my father because I live with him." In his simplicity, the boy defined the role about as well as anybody could. There is a lot of blank to fill in. Yet the blanks are already filled. Perhaps the stepfather can just write his name above the line, being careful not to cross anything out. An addition, not a substitution.

The stepfather knows he has a life-forming role to play. Yet he is the someone more, not the replacement. Somewhere, whether in fact or memory, the original father lives on, and the stepfather must come to terms with his feelings about the prior husband and father.

THE FORMER SPOUSE

Nancy was talking in her sleep. Bruce turned to listen. Earlier that night she'd called him by her first husband's name—Carl!

The one-syllable stab. It was the third time she'd done it when they were making love. Made you wonder. The bastard was probably one hell of a stud. One thing for sure: *he* didn't wear himself out working.

What was she saying all tangled up in the sheet? "Without a passport . . . even the furniture knows . . ." Incredible woman. Dreaming in some kind of poetry. She sounded in anguish. The whole business must hurt her more than it did him. He wished he could spare her some of the pain, do better by Bobby for her, keep his ex from needling her—somehow balance the whole thing better.

There she went again. ". . . Carl . . ."

Carl! Damn it! He had a furious urge to punch the guy, roaming the world scot free while *he* had his feet held to the fire with both sets of kids.

Then, occasionally, along would come Carl. He seldom saw Bobby or Kim, but when he did, every day was a circus. The man was a pied piper with kids. They adored him. Hell, why not?—he could spend all day flying a kite. . . .

Dr. Oshiver Fisher speaks of the need for the couple to view the former spouse in the same way, preferably with indifference. Should there be too great hostility or too great friendliness, the spouse has not been relegated to history and the current marriage will have a poor prognosis for success. The past, she says, belongs to the individuals; the future to the new couple.

While the ex-husband may be relegated to the past, the father cannot be. He remains in the present and future of the children, and as such is still in the picture.

Stepfathers can bring about positive gains in the family by making it a rule never to run down the father to the children. Best of all (and it isn't easy) is to forge a working relationship with the father where the child is concerned. If the two men can sit down and talk about the child's problems, those problems will stand a chance of being solved. Even if the father is trying to turn the children against their stepfather, a talk may still be worth a try.

Where the father is dead the stepfather must take over the duties of the father. He is almost certain to have to contend with an idealized memory. Again, he has to give the child space and time.

"I never talked against their father," one stepfather told us. "I always said nice things about him. To say anything critical would be self-indulgent and undignified. It would be hurting somebody pointlessly. When the kids get older, they find out for themselves.

"Also, I never tried to take their father's place. He was a nice and thoroughly kind man, though not very smart. He lived in the same suburban town as we do; I encouraged the children to see him.

"I did one thing that I know enhanced my relationship with the kids. It had meaning at the time, and I knew why I was doing it. Their father had remarried and was once again separated or divorced just before Christmas. On Christmas Eve we traditionally went out to dinner and then trimmed the tree. I invited their father to join us. The evening was reasonably comfortable because the relationship was comfortable. The kids have never forgotten it.

"Sure, at times I had jealousy way down, but I would never let the kids know it. I mean I loved those kids so much I would really like them to think of me as their total father. They do think of me as their father, and unless they're introducing me to somebody who knows their father, they introduce me as their dad. That means a lot to me—and it would never have happened if I'd tried to force it."

By including the father, by deliberately attempting not to replace him, this man became more, not less, of a father figure to his stepchildren. He can't change the fact that the children are't his, and he hasn't tried to. He has settled for a good relationship with the children he loves—and has gotten love in return.

THE MONEY RIDDLE

Stepfathers are confronted with a money riddle. Frequently, they must support two families. Or support one, and be partially supported in another. Either way it doesn't bode well. Finances figure high in the causes of the breakdown of remarriages.

Often the wife brings into a second marriage some financial support either through child support or through working. It may be a pittance, or it may be enough to support her half, or more. Not being able to contribute the major support to the new family, or merely the fact of another man's contribution, can undermine a stepfather.

One stepfather explains, "The father would tell the children exactly what he was paying in child support and tell them to refuse the hot dogs we gave them. He told them to ask for lamb chops.

"The kids would want to take riding lessons. Their mother would say, 'You can't take them unless Daddy will pay for them.' I [the stepfather] would have been happy to pay for them if they only had asked me."

When the wife works, she may feel that she's working to support her husband's prior family. Whether or not she is, she may perceive it that way. One husband resolved his wife's bitterness by suggesting she save from her salary the amount he paid out to his former wife in alimony. It was her own private spending fund, and she felt better.

A man often finds himself supporting two households and having both women feel that he's not doing well by them.

"The keeping of the two households and six children is a huge financial burden. Even a person with a high income like I have is strapped. The extras and the school bills are eating me up.

"What frustrates me most is the inability to get across to all six children and wife that funds are not unlimited. It becomes a terrible balancing act as to who, from which family, is going to have to give up what.

"On top of it all, I live in a constant concern that my ex will be coming back at me for more child support because of inflation. Periodically, I get nasty registered letters from lawyers with lists of things which she claims that I owe her that are not in the contract."

The current wife resents what he pays to the former family, and the former wife resents what he gives to his present family. He may find both wives using money as a weapon and as a means to test loyalties and love.

Unless there is plenty to go around, and sometimes even if

there is, the wife may try to direct the money away from the prior family and toward her own. If the prior wife is bitter and nasty, she helps the new wife's scene, for she has provided a means for the man to feel justified in cutting her off.

The question of wills was constantly brought up by stepfathers. When the relationship had gone well, a stepfather would frequently tell us that he had included his stepchildren along with his own children in the will. One could say that in step the will is used as a barometer of feelings. The ultimate triumph of certain wives is to have the others excluded from the will. The ultimate triumph of certain children and former wives is to have the current wife cut back to precisely her legal widow's share. Matters are going even further these days. A somewhat current case in point is that of Jacqueline Onassis who at the death of her husband had to stand by a premarital agreement which gave her only a fraction of her legal widow's share.

Money in step can become a heavy emotional weapon, and the stepfather can be caught in the crossfire. His ex-wife may use it with his children as a funnel for her hatred, revenge, or continued dependency. His wife may use it in her ways to test the crossed lines and alliances. He may begin to look at them all as vultures. He has to be extremely mature in his handling of the money as well as the demands, or he can be trampled by the endless requirements and miss the point of it all.

THE RITES OF PASSAGE

Peter Cohen pushed the lighted buttons on his phone, dealing and dispensing with calls and secretaries. As he talked he stood up and walked around the desk. A smile crossed his face, and he reached out his hand and said: "No more calls. Jonathan and I will be going out to lunch shortly. Thank you, Mary."

Through all the adversities of the business downturn, Peter Cohen had made the right decisions. He was rich and respected. He knew that. If he could only feel that good about his family.

They were some team of his, hers, and ours—five in all, and all boys. Three of his, living less than an hour away, hers, Jonathan, 18, and their young Paul. Often they were all at home. Sometimes he felt like the grand patriarch of a large and lovely family.

Other times he felt like the keeper of a bunch of blubbering, belligerent adolescents.

His notions on raising children were different from Diedre's He was Jewish. She wasn't. He could never think of a child becoming anything but a professional person. The child must be guided toward becoming something.

Diedre was so different, so easygoing. Her notion is to bear the child and get it to become independent as soon as possible.

Oh, he went along with that, now . . . Just as long as the kid becomes a doctor . . . calls home every week . . . and let's me know what he's been eating.

After lunch Peter came back to his office visibly stunned. The kid had actually stood up and threatened him in the restaurant . . . letting go with this barrage about, "How awful I was to his younger half-brother the other night at dinner . . . and when he went away there would be no one to defend Paul. Threatening that I had better stop treating Paul like a jerk . . . and that *I* had wrecked too many dinners with my temper tantrums . . . And that he'd been scared of me long enough. And now he'd be going away, and if that stuff happened again when he came home on the next holiday, he'd haul off and hit me. After all I've done! His father doesn't pay for anything, and I'm paying for college and he's giving me hell.

"God, how could Jonathan say these things. Oh, each of my own has gone through a period of being anti-father. But their mother has done every possible thing to disturb their relationship with me. She had them call their new stepfather "Dad" right from the beginning. That was the worst. I guess they felt they had to choose.

"That puny kid who was so dear when I married Diedre. He'd hold on to my hand and want to go for walks. He was so eager to have a man around. The poor child had never seen his father. He would answer the door when the United Parcel man came and ask, 'Are you my Daddy?'

"The most difficult thing about starting at 4 instead of birth was developing Jonathan's toughness toward the world. It's important for kids to learn how to be tough, and certainly his mother wouldn't teach him.

"Well look at it. Jonathan is now a very tough kid. He can

accomplish great physical feats and has great stamina. He has tremendous curiosity. And a few years ago he actually turned around and became a good student.

"And he just slugged me verbally. I wonder who he learned that from . . ."

For all parents, the rites of passage can be jolting: the child throws over the parents on his way to adulthood. For the step-parent, the necessary struggle can feel particularly unjust.

BRUCE

He'd run into Ross and Slater on the train that night. The damn train had gotten stuck again, and after three martinis they'd gotten to talking. They had a lot in common. All of them were remarried with kids. Slater had recently married a woman with three kids. He said it was like trying to learn to swim from the deep end rather than the shallow. He'd never had kids before and had little idea about how to go about it. There'd been trouble as soon as they got home from the honeymoon.

Ross had said not to worry about it, that it would all work out in about five years. Slater had ordered another round of drinks on that one and Ross had said, "Yeah, that's what I thought when a shrink I was seeing told me that. But you'd be surprised. Just hang in there."

Funny. Most guys say everything's okay, so you figure you're the only one with any major problems. They probably just won't talk about it.

Driving home from the station, he thought about his two stepkids. Kim had been natural and friendly from the beginning. She'd loved having him a part of the family. But Bobby was another story. God, the tides of hostility that flowed from that boy! It was as though the kid had a snake inside his head, coiling and uncoiling. When it was coiled, he was sullen. When it uncoiled, he struck. The anger was almost better than the sourness.

Admittedly, Bobby was getting better, but at the time they were married, the kid had been weird. Cry like a girl if he hurt himself. Didn't have the faintest idea what good sportsmanship was. The boy had irritated him, had embarrassed him, frankly. And Nancy hadn't seen that there was anything wrong. He'd tried to toughen him up, but it was hard not being able to start at the beginning and having to buck Nancy all the way.

Kim had always had a sense of her own destination. She had more than that to tell the truth. She'd always been a little flirt, a little coquette. And helpful. There wasn't anything she wouldn't do for him. It was impossible not to respond. And a bit tricky too, now that she was developing into a little woman.

She was actually competing with Nancy, but Nancy didn't seem to mind it. In fact, she encouraged it. According to Nancy, Kim was learning how to be a woman, how to relate to men. She was practicing it out on her old stepdad.

Just let his own daughter Margie try the same thing, however, and Nancy would fly into a childlike rage! Obviously the same rules didn't apply.

It was hard to keep the fantasies down. Kim was running around with tee shirts and no bra—now there was a girl who couldn't get by going braless. And lately she'd taken to greeting him at the door, holding her face up for a kiss on the lips. He'd give it to her on the cheek, but still . . . At least she wasn't his own flesh-and-blood daughter.

But she was his daughter! She really was. Maybe more so. She'd patterned herself after him—hard-working, capable. She was his daughter, a special gift, and he loved her. Still, it was difficult not to be turned on. He wondered if any guys actually slipped and got in trouble that way.

SEXUALITY AND STEP

The absence of clearly defined sexual taboos in step relationships intensifies the normal problems of resolving and properly directing sexual impulses. The incest taboo is by no means firmly extended to step relationships. That is unfortunate because, whatever its original purpose, the taboo enables people to live together intimately with, hopefully, a minimum of sexual rivalries.

Some mothers see potential incest in every stepfather-stepdaughter flirtation. And some stepfathers and stepdaughters do become involved in highly sexualized interchanges.

Sexual rivalry is common in step, and exhibits itself between stepparents and stepchildren of any age.

Frequently, upon remarriage a daughter will begin to see her mother in a different way. She has been alerted to her mother's sexuality as her mother dated, courted, and married. Her response can be one of competitiveness or hostility: she will vie for the stepfather's attention, or busy herself putting her mother down. Her feelings often are further complicated by the belief that her mother has betrayed or driven out her own father.

One teenage stepdaughter was extremely candid about her feelings at the time her mother remarried: "There I was with my own sex drives, and I wasn't getting anywhere. Why should my mother, of all people, be getting hers with her new husband?"

A stepfather tells how he reacted: "She was impossible with her mother, constantly dumping on her—and, at the same time, never leaving her alone, always hanging around the kitchen or wherever her mother happened to be. She didn't direct her hostility at me, but it infuriated me to see her going after her mother. I thought, 'Who is this little twerp to put down the woman I love?' "

ROADBLOCKS TO INTIMACY

Many stepfathers feel that they are prevented by their stepchildren from getting close to them—in a variety of ways. They tell us that the children set up roadblocks to intimacy and warmth.

The family is out on a picnic. Everybody's having a wonderful time, when all of a sudden one of the stepchildren will say, "Mommy, do you remember when you and Daddy and we went on a picnic at the beach? How much fun we had."

Often the stepfather tries to cross over the unspoken barriers only to be rebuffed.

The stepfather says, "Hello, Johnny."

No answer.

The mother says, "Johnny, say hello to Paul."

Johnny says, "Oh, hello, I didn't see you."

The stepfather is six feet two and weighs two hundred pounds.

The coldness, the barriers to warmth, the sudden shifts in mood are painful and discouraging to a stepfather. The remedy lies, again, in understanding where the behavior comes from. It goes back to the old business of troubled loyalties. Perhaps a child wants to deny the existence of the stepfather (Stepfather is where Dad should be). Sometimes when a stepchild turns a cold shoulder, that's the very moment he's feeling a rush of love. It's just too scary sometimes for the child. He's lost one parent and can be terrified of losing the only remaining parent. Maybe he wants Mother all to himself.

It is important for a stepfather not to press—and not to take the behavior as a personal insult.

WITHDRAWING FROM THE CHILD

Frequently, of course, it's the stepfather himself who sets up the barrier to closeness. He may dislike the child or resent the intrusion of this symbol of his wife's former marriage and love. He wishes the child were not there—and shows it.

The child says hello.

The stepfather walks on by.

The child blurts out, "I made two goals in hockey today."

The stepfather turns to his wife and says, "The traffic was terrible on the way home tonight."

The child says, "Let me show you my magic show."

The stepfather doesn't look up from his newspaper.

The child is hurt—and so is the mother. She can't easily forgive the stepfather's indifference. She knows her child's ego is being undermined. She may try so hard to force a better relationship that the stepfather withdraws even further.

Should the stepfather find himself retreating at the sight of the child, he may find that things go better with the child when Mom's not around. "I didn't like the kid much at all," one stepfather told us. "Always doing God knows what for his mother's attention. She would sleep late on Sundays, and the boy and I would drive into town to get the paper. We started talking and laughing together. He wasn't half bad without her. I started taking him places with me and we did a few things together at home. It wasn't too long before I got to really enjoy the kid."

The male figure in the household is essential to the child. Should the stepfather withdraw from the fray and withhold stepfatherly attention, he may find himself emotionally paying for it down the road, through his wife. She too may withdraw from him. Whether she does or not, the stepfather will miss out on the rewards that come with involvement.

But the involvement, as with one's own children, needs to be taken with a sense of the child's own individuality, difference, and independent identity.

One stepfather explains: "My fantasy was that a stepfather was a duplication of a father. It was a marvelously naïve idea, that I would be Pygmalion, that I would immediately adopt my stepdaughter into me.

"I wanted to love her. When I married her mother, I married her. I had this great desire to absorb her into this marvelous me.

"I slowly had to go through a phase of separating her from me. It was my separation. I had to learn not to try to be the perfect father, not to try so hard, not to feel that I owed so much.

"The most maturing thing for me was to accept this other person in her complexity. I had to try not to make the child a part of my own ego. I had to unhook my own ego."

BRUCE

The rewards are there—in the long run the involvement can pay off.

"Hey, Pops," Bobby called out, "how about letting me take the car tonight?"

The bastard's probably just calling me that to get the car, Bruce thought; but something turned over in his heart, and he threw Bobby the keys.

The changes lately. Could this be the same kid that used to drive him up the wall? Bobby was working at school now. He was beginning to show signs of a genuine loyalty. Bruce had recently heard from a friend that Bobby had been bragging about him.

Their conversations had become lively. They'd talk about all kinds of things together—sports, business, sex, ideas, anything. The kid sometimes sounded like him. The voice, sometimes, the ways of joking, even some of the same ideas.

They'd have fun doing things together. All of them. Kim too. What a gem she was. She'd become a real beauty, and she still was the same sweet, sensitive kid. And now she had a hot and heavy boyfriend.

The kids were growing up, and he was proud of them. He and Nancy, for all their troubles, were doing a decent job of it. Now that the kids were older, they weren't in the way all the time. Sure he and Nancy still fought about them, but it was different now. Nancy would worry over some little thing one of them did and blow it into a big problem. He'd help her see it in proportion.

He still wished his own girls could live with them. And yet, come to think of it, if anything happened to Nancy and him, he'd feel the same way about being separated from Bobby and Kim. Better not to think about that.

You know, Ross had been right. If you could hang in there long enough—years, it had been now—you got to a point where you began to feel right about it all.

He figured that being a stepfather, no, being a father, whether they were your own or somebody else's—was being the man in the house. You had to be there for them to know you, enjoy you, fight against you if they had to. Just being there was more than half the battle.

6

The Child in Step

DONNY WOULD RUN along between both parents, each arm reaching high—one to Mommy, one to Daddy. Then one, two, three, swwwiiiinnnnggg, Donny would swoop through the air. "Again! Again!" he'd shout. One, two, threeee . . .

Sometimes they'd go to the beach. Daddy would take him out in the water and hold him tight while the waves rolled around them. He'd laugh while the white water smashed around Daddy and him. Nothing bad could happen when Daddy was there. Back to the blanket where Mommy would have lunch, sandwiches and cold drinks. Before they packed up to leave, Mommy and Daddy would swing him in the blanket, one on each side, and toss him in the air. Whoowee!

It was all warm and happy. Mommy laughed a lot. Daddy would come home early and play bear on the rug, grumbling bear noises and rubbing him with his prickly whiskers. Daddy could do everything and would show him how.

There came the time, then, when Mommy stopped laughing and Daddy stopped coming home early. Bear! Bear! he'd shout, but Daddy and Mommy weren't hearing him.

In the night he'd wake up scared. He'd dream that Mommy and Daddy were fighting. But still the voices went on. The dream wasn't over. "Daddy! Daddy! Mommy! Mommy! Mommy-daddymommydaddymommydaddymommydaddy!"

"There, there." They would both rush into the room and

stroke him and hold him tight. Bad dream! There, there, the little boy's all right. Clutching something furry in his little fist, he'd go back to sleep.

Then, one afternoon, he heard them fighting in the next room. Low voices getting louder and softer, all tough and edgy like sandpaper. He couldn't move; he stood there listening, holding his breath. Clear as a cannon, he heard Daddy: "How can you ask me to give up that wonderful boy?"

The world stopped, and somewhere in the void he heard the word "Divorce! divorce! divorce!" crashing like so many waves of disaster. He'd never heard it before, he didn't know what it meant, but he knew it was horrible.

He was staring at his toy chest with the circus animals, red and yellow, marching bravely around it. Time stopped. The next thing he knew, Mommy and Daddy, together, were both holding him, and he heard himself shrieking a high-pitched, tearing scream.

THE LOSS

A child's world is his family. When that breaks, his sense of self and his security are shattered. Most children in one way or another have been held up by both parents. Mother and father on either side hold a hand and swing the child over the rough spots as over the curb. When one of them leaves, the child is yanked out of proportion. Now he's supported on one side, and the other side is left hanging.

A child handles the loss in different ways. Many don't show their deep feelings, but the loss is imprinted within them and colors the rest of their lives.

In fairy tales, the hard time for the stepchild starts when the father remarries. Anne Simon refutes this in *Stepchild in the Family:* "The hard time for the poor stepchild began once upon a time when he had a mother and father together . . . and then did not."

Ms. Simon goes on to say that the process of learning to love and be loved was interrupted, that while few adults can take death or divorce with composure, no child can. She writes of the terror and confusion cutting deep, and the scar being slow to heal.

The memory of that confusion and that pain is part of any stepchild's heritage. It is the load the child lugs into the remarriage.

The degree to which any of us, child or adult, is secure, anxious, or distressed is determined to a large extent by the accessibility and responsiveness of our principal attachment figure, the person we care about the most. If he or she is there —or, we believe, will be there to respond to us when needed, we'll be okay.

With most children, the principal attachment figure is the mother, although it could be the father or another person. The child may or may not have lost his principal figure through divorce or death. But he has lost one parent and fears the loss of the other. If one can leave, cannot the other leave also? A child growing up with no confidence that his caretaking figure will be truly available or dependable may well tend to view the world as comfortless or unpredictable. Some children respond by shrinking from the world; others by doing battle with it.

What happens to the child depends to a large degree on the remaining parent and future stepparent. If they are supportive, nurturing, and available, the loss and insecurity will be minimized. Unfortunately, the greatest need for reassurance after divorce or death comes at a time when the remaining parent is also undermined by loss and change. That parent's fear, loss, and loneliness may well be communicated to the child. Stepchildren have told us of the aloneness and helplessness they felt through their mothers, before remarriage:

"You try to block it out and go on, to be like the next guy. You know if you walk around with your head down and shoulders shrunk, you're going to get it. Other kids are like sharks—they sense that you're wounded or floundering.

"But my mother was so completely miserable for so many years, all her desolation came through to me. We were all so much weaker without my father.

"People treated us differently. Mother was not invited to the parties in the neighborhood. She was hurt by the reactions of people. When people did do something, you felt it was out of kindness and pity."

Children certainly pick up on the parent's unhappiness.

"Why doesn't my daddy live here any more?" Donny wanted to know. "Why doesn't my daddy come home? Where is my daddy, anyway?"

Donny didn't understand. It didn't make sense. Daddy had left Donny. Donny wondered what he had done to make Daddy leave him. Didn't Daddy love him?

Mommy took him to nursery school, with all the children, all the wonderful toys, but Donny could think of only one thing. Would Mommy come back to pick him up? What if *Mommy* went away? He'd crawl under the table sometimes and wait for her. Then she'd come, and he'd know he'd made it through one more day. . . .

The child needs explanations that square with reality. He also needs assurance and reassurance—at separation and right through the remarriage—that his needs will be met, that there will be food and shelter, that there will be somebody to take care of him.

He *doesn't* need to share in problems about which he can do nothing, like mother's money problems, her gripes against father, her fears of not being able to manage. The burden is too big for the child to bear. It will only drag him down.

As adults we often fail to understand how a child is experiencing an event. We tend to view children as miniature adults. They aren't. A young child, especially, views his world totally egocentrically. He sees things as happening only in relation to himself.

Thus, if a child's parent dies, the child may somehow believe that this parent deserted him on purpose. Or, if he had angry thoughts against that parent, he may subconsciously believe that his thoughts evoked the death.

The same is true in the case of divorce. It is hard for the child to see that he was not the reason for the divorce, that neither his wishes, nor his deeds, nor his failure to act brought about the divorce. Unexpressed guilt is one of the many emotions that plague the child at the loss of a parent.

Donny was very angry with Mommy for sending Daddy away, and yet, when he would scream at her, Mommy would say it wasn't her fault. Donny figured it must be his fault, or Daddy wouldn't have left.

Sometimes he'd dream that Daddy had come home, but when he'd wake up in the morning, it would just be him and Mommy. Sometimes a friend of Mommy's would be there. He'd be nice to him, put Donny's feet on his shoes and walk him around. But just when Donny got to count on him he'd go away too. Donny and Mommy would both get sad and be alone again. What was wrong with him and Mommy? Why wouldn't anyone stay?

One day Mommy told Donny that Daddy was coming to see him. Donny was excited. Daddy had been bad to leave Donny and Mommy for so long, but Donny wouldn't say anything. He'd be good and he'd promise to be very, very good, and maybe Daddy would stay.

"You're growing up to be a fine boy," Daddy told Donny. "I'm proud of you."

And then it just slipped out. "If you're proud of me, why don't you stay here with me?"

"I can't stay, Donny. Mommy and I are divorced. I wish I could see you more often, but when my business moved to California, I had to go. I'm sorry we have to live so far apart."

"Maybe Mommy and I could come and live there with you. I'll be very good."

"Donny, Mommy and I won't be living together any more. Mommy and I couldn't get along. We both love you and will always love you. But we won't live together."

"If you both love me, then you'll try to get along! You'll try to live together!"

"No, Donny, I'm sorry but we can't. I know it's hard on you. It's hard on me, and it's hard on Mommy. But we just all have to be brave. I want you to know that I'm behind you all the way. If there's anything I can do to help you, I'll do it."

"How can you help me when you aren't here? What if my wagon handle comes off again?"

"It's hard, Donny. At those times you'll have to look to Mommy for help. But I'll be there if you need me in a big way. You can telephone me. And I want you to know that I send Mommy money for you and her to live on."

Donny felt relieved. But, when Daddy took him home, Mommy and Daddy started yelling at each other. Mommy cried. She told Daddy there wasn't enough money. Daddy said she wasted money. Mommy said his checks were late, and what was she supposed to do? Daddy said she was lying. Daddy said . . . Mommy said . . .

Donny ran out of the room and hid under the covers on his bed. He put his hands over his ears.

"Stop! Stop!" he whispered. But the fighting continued, almost as though it were inside him, the two parts of him pulling apart and banging together again. . . .

Whether in the marriage or out of the marriage, a child becomes caught in his parents' fights. When parents are in conflict, they don't confine their fights to themselves. Some of the tension inevitably spills over onto the child, who begins to realize that he is part of the battle.

Parents who think they have concealed the fighting from the child are fooling themselves, says Connecticut psychologist Dr. David Ulrich.

One way or the other, parents will triangle the child into their fights.

A child's tension will go up when the parents are fighting. If the child breaks in, the parents' tension goes down; but the child's stays the same. It is almost automatic, Dr. Ulrich says, that a child will intervene to defuse the conflict by drawing attention to himself. Comes a remarriage, and the child carries part of this patterning into the stepfamily.

The identity of a child lies with both biological parents. When the two of them hack away at each other—sometimes in front of the child, sometimes through the child—he cannot help being confused and conflicted.

If either of the parents is denigrated, the child feels diminished. Parents who put each other down do so at the cost of the child's own self-esteem.

It's easy enough to say that one ought never to speak against a child's parent. Yet a child needs explanations—for divorce, for neglect, for other parental behavior. Whitewashing doesn't meet the child's needs. The answer lies in telling as much of the truth as is appropriate and necessary without unnecessarily running down or blaming the other parent.

By the time a child becomes a stepchild his security and self-esteem may have been shaken in any number of ways. Not only the feeling of having his family split apart, but the fear of future breakups may plague him. The anger, sadness, or shakiness of the remaining parent may have been absorbed by the child, who *learns* through that parent's way of handling crisis and loss. Parental neglect, fighting, and bad-mouthing all may have conspired against the child and the family that he assumed would go on forever he now knows can end.

But time washes us, and we grow and go on learning. At any given stage of development, a child can recover and recoup losses. His friends, teachers, parents, stepparents, others can pull him out. Or he can pull himself out.

Parents and stepparents like to believe that the solutions lie in remarriage: mending and healing will take place as the family becomes whole again. We begin anew, and the prognosis is rosy. Well, the kids aren't so sure.

REACTIONS TO REMARRIAGE

"I was nineteen when my father got married and in my twenties and already married when my mother remarried," Jeannette remembers. "I was happy for them. I'd had each of them separately to myself for almost a decade. Yet my father knew it wouldn't be easy for me. He called me to come up to his office.

" 'What is it, Daddy?' "

" 'Tell you when you get here.'

"Every time I think about it, the scene comes sharply into focus. He sat in his big chair. I sat in a straight-backed chair. He pulled my chair close to him. Gave me a hug. Head close to mine, he told me.

" 'Hilda and I have married.'

"The room froze—I think I got a fever. Every detail of that moment remains sharply in my memory: the red-backed chairs, the gray conference table, the way my father leaned forward . . .

"I said that I hoped he would be happy, that I was glad he was married. I hugged him. I said he needed to be married. He'd been single and going out with so many women for so long. I said that I knew it would be good, that she'd be good for him.

"Inside I was terrified. I thought I'd lose him to her. And I did. For years I'd been the primary woman in his life. We'd done a lot together—trips to Europe, business dinners, the theater. Now he'd be doing all that with her. He did. Of course I was welcome in their home, but it was all different now."

Donny didn't like it either. Mother told him one day when they were driving in the car, "I have wonderful news. You're going to have a new daddy. Uncle George and I are getting married next month."

Donny thought of his daddy out in California. He wondered if he'd still see him as much. A kind of sadness and panic began inside him. Then a hope. He said, "Maybe Uncle George won't want to get married."

Mommy laughed. "Sure he will, Donny. It's something we both decided."

"Well, you didn't ask me! I don't want a new daddy. I don't want Uncle George."

"Of course you do, Donny," Mommy said. "You'll see. We're going to move to a new house. You'll go to a new school. Just wait. Everything will be marvelous."

"I don't want a new *anything*. I want us to stay the way we are. I hate Uncle George!"

Donny's mother was stunned. She loved George, and she was certain Donny liked him.

"Donny, of course you don't hate Uncle George. Don't you understand? Life will be a lot easier for us now."

She proceeded to paint a rosy picture of the future. The better it sounded, the more confused Donny got. He did like

Uncle George, but he didn't want a new daddy. He already had a daddy, and he wanted him back.

He remembered the first time he'd heard the word "divorce," standing there by his red and yellow toy box. Maybe it would happen again. He didn't know. He didn't even know what he wanted. Mommy kept telling him about the good things. Back and forth. He tried not to listen but to just watch the windshield wipers going left and right. When he didn't say anything more, Mommy figured she'd convinced him. And Donny kept feeling that awful fear in his stomach. . . .

Donny's fear was not so much the loss of his mother to his new stepfather, but the replacement of his father by his stepfather. Had his mother understood this, she would have assured Donny that George was to be a stepdaddy, not a new daddy. She would have reassured Donny right then that he would still see, have, and love his own daddy. As it was, she allowed the situation to get set up in Donny's mind as an either/or proposition, which virtually guaranteed his resistance.

TALKING ABOUT IT

Any discussion of remarriage needs to allow some open space for a child's responses, some acceptance of his feelings whether they be pro or con. Donny's mother did not allow him any expressions of his feelings.

She did a natural thing. She had to believe in the future of the merger, or she wouldn't be getting married. Her own positive beliefs, however, didn't prepare Donny for the inevitable conflicts to come. By pointing to some of the negatives as well as the positives, she might have been able to inoculate him emotionally to the tough realities of step.

She might have done it this way:

"Donny, Uncle George and I have decided to get married. I hope that you will enjoy having him for your stepfather. Of course there may be certain things you won't like about him, and that's natural—there are things you don't like about me. Don't feel bad about it."

She could stop here. Later, over a period of time, she could introduce new elements for consideration, pausing each time to accept Donny's responses and hear them through.

"I'm very happy about this marriage, Donny. There will be more people in your life, and life will be easier for us. But it may not be easy for you in the beginning. Uncle George will take up more of my time. But he'll also be spending more time with you."

"You'll have a new stepbrother and a new stepsister. Sometimes it will be fun, and sometimes it will be hard to share. I will be spending part of my time with them too, and sometimes we will all be doing things together.

"You know I love you and will always love you because you are my child. Together we will try to get along with all the new people in our lives, and I believe we can."

We asked Nicky Roosevelt, Ruth's youngest stepson (fourteen) to write down some advice for a child about to become a stepchild. This is what he wrote:

"You must look into the new person who is going to make you a stepchild to the extent of seeing right through his or her thought patterns and personality. It may look good or it may look bad, but you better damn well make sure it's good, or future life will be extremely sad. Realize what effects this person will have in your life, think into the future to some extent, think if your life will flow straight or bent. Talk to your parents and *say what you think!* Don't be scared to give a piece of your mind, for this plays the part of an important link.

"Being a stepchild does not make you any different from what you once were or are in the present. You are treated the same and sometimes better if you are an only child. Although if your stepfather or stepmother also has children, making them your stepbrothers and sisters makes things different. In this case you may find that the parent or parents will not treat you equally but tend to pick out favorites—this is what some people I talk to seem to think in this situation. Stepchildren have said to me, 'My dad or mom used to do more with me and buy more for me until my stepmother or father stepped in.' This is a pessimistic side often given. As for the optimistic point of view, many are happy they gained a new person or new people to be around. There are a lot of hardships and tough situations here and there, but as they say, 'When the going gets tough—the tough get going.' But for the new stepchild, remember, it's all at the beginning. Say what you think while you have the chance."

We asked Nicky's stepbrother, Graham Anthony (Ruth's son, eleven) to give us the best and the worst of being a stepchild. Without hesitation he said, "The worst is that you see less of your other parent. The best is that you have somebody extra who cares about you."

Step is good news and bad news. The good news is that there's more; the bad news is that there's less.

Most stepchildren think they should have a voice in whether a parent remarries and whom he or she marries. The feeling is understandable. Decisions are being made that alter the content and quality of a child's whole life. Nevertheless, the marriage —and the decision—are the parent's. The parent cannot put the child in a position of yeaing or naying the remarriage. Allowing him to feel that he has control over the decision can give him a false feeling of power or helplessness about the marital relationship. Neither the marriage decision nor the success of the marriage is the child's responsibility.

That is not to say that the child should not have an opportunity to express his opinions and feelings about the marriage or the proposed marriage partner. The child's feelings are important and should be brought out and accepted.

Dr. Ulrich cautions the parent to wait after death or divorce before remarrying. The child needs time to mourn the loss, to adjust to the transitions, to become fully acquainted with the new partner. This would be one of the few instances, he says, where he would counsel a parent to put his own needs behind those of a child. If the child's reactions to the remarriage are too strong, it may be that the parent should postpone the marriage for six months or so while the child and future stepparent have an opportunity to build a relationship.

The children should be aware of the impending marriage beforehand, not have the announcement come as a spectacular event. If it bursts as a surprise, that's too fast for comfort.

Teenagers' common complaint about the remarriage of a parent, Dr. Ulrich says, is that it happened too fast.

THE FEARS

The event of remarriage often stirs up in the child the old feelings from the crisis of separation. Old fears come alive, and new fears join forces with them.

Who am I now? Where do I belong? Does my parent remarrying still love me? Will I lose my mother/father to this person he/she is remarrying? Can I like this new stepparent and still love my other parent? A whirl of uncertainties surrounds the child. The fears are there. Usually they are reinforced rather than calmed in the new marriage.

On the one hand, in the excitement of the marriage, too little attention may be paid the children. The parent is busy with new arrangements, building relationships with new stepchildren, pleasing and spending time with the new spouse, perhaps even away on an extended honeymoon—and, often, operating under the assumption that the old relationship with the children is a constant that will take care of itself.

A child may read it that he counts less now, that his status will go down. Other people seem to be more important now. Though he doesn't want to believe it, a child may begin to perceive the parent as somebody he can't count on the way he used to.

On the other hand, a child may be put in too central a position. Too much attention may be paid to him. Parent and stepparent may bend over backward to include the child. He begins to feel omnipotent in the new marriage or crowded by the stepparent and parent.

The new stepparent may overdiscipline, overdo, or just plain overwhelm in an effort to build the instant relationship. The child feels forced. Here is this new person that the child will have to get along with, like it or not. Sometimes the child doesn't like it.

A child may be worried about betraying the original parent.

Without willing it or understanding it, he may cut off affection for the new stepparent, feeling that such affection would be disloyal. The inner mechanism of loyalty to one's own can squelch any developing love, or surround that love with guilt. It works something like "Thou shalt have no other Love before Me." It is a form of patriotism or chauvinism; nothing is as good as, or shall take the place of, one's own—motherland or fatherland, mother or father.

The child may act resentful and hostile, startling the parent or stepparent, who sees no apparent reason for such sudden negative behavior.

One mother explained her son's reactions to her marriage. "It had been a long, hard time between marriages. My son Mark and I lived in a small apartment in a poor part of the city. I worked and dated and did the best I could to give Mark the time and attention he needed, but life was difficult and uncertain.

"When at last I was getting remarried—and ecstatic about the marriage—I expected Mark to share this joy. He was fond of my future husband and loved the prospect of living in the country. We had a beautiful new home, and I would have plenty of time for family life.

"One day shortly before the marriage, as we drove up the driveway of what was to be our new home, Mark suddenly said, 'I'd rather live in Sacramento with my father.'

" 'How can you be so ungrateful!' I shouted as I jammed on the brakes, turned around and slapped him.

"It was years before I realized what he was saying then. It wasn't that he was unappreciative of our new life. He liked it, but loyalty to his father prevented him from allowing the easy flow of delight. Even now, I'm sure that, could he bring his father and me back together again, that would be his first choice. In spite of our marvelous life."

The feelings of betrayal may be reinforced by either the new stepparent or the parents. The parent or the counterpart stepparent (father and stepfather) may show insecurity regarding the other. Either may encourage the child to reject the other, or set up a competition for superiority that conveys to the child the necessity of making a choice.

Dr. Ulrich explains a phenomenon that we wish we'd understood from the beginning of our step marriages. A child, he says, is likely to approach the stepparent with ingrained patterns of reaction to parenting. If, for example, he felt and behaved a certain way toward his mother, he is likely to treat the stepmother the same way. A good relationship with the mother would predispose the child to a good relationship with the stepmother.

The same with the father and stepfather. Say the parental breakup occurred with the mother derogating the father. The chances are that the child will treat the stepfather the same way. If the child likes the father, he will be more predisposed to like the stepfather.

Some other authorities we talked with agreed that the patterns of the child in interacting with the stepparent would be similar to his interactions with that parent, but only to the extent that the individuals were similar. If a parent had, for example, been for some reason not nurturing of the child, and if the stepparent was warm and nurturing, the child might ultimately develop a quite different pattern of interaction.

THE CHANGES

Whatever the child's pattern, the family is his world, and the world changes overnight.

Suddenly, here is stepfather. He used to visit Mom and bring the kids chocolate candy. He used to take them every so often to ball games, on picnics, and out to dinner. Now he's moved in; and he's taken over Mom. He sets up a bunch of new rules which he enforces, nicely or not. Or maybe he doesn't. Maybe he just moves in and ignores them. And he brings his bratty kids around on weekends.

Sometimes he comes in and he charms the whole family. Grumpy old Mom is suddenly all smiles and nice again. Everybody is charged with new vitality. The family style of living is immediately upgraded. Maybe the stepbrothers or sisters are great new friends to have. It's like those old movies when things suddenly turn out right. Stepdad is seen as a white knight. In this sort of situation, the kids may do their best to work at the merger, to see that it lasts.

But always, when Mom remarries, a lot of things change. The family name changes. Usually the child's name doesn't change. Suddenly, he has a different name from his mother, from his family. His very name indicates that he is outside the family, somehow not an integral part of this new alliance. Family traditions change. The way things had always been done is now different. The shared past is not shared by all.

Even the numbers change, the size and structure of the family. An only child can become one of three. The youngest loses position to three younger. The oldest now has one older. And so forth. To add a new parent and brothers and sisters, midstream in growing up, is a heavy adjustment.

Houses, schools, bedrooms, places at the table, desks, closets—anything may change. All too frequently, a stepchild gets the feeling of not belonging. Everybody in the house may feel the same way; usually it's not talked about but acted out.

Because of the disruptions in the child's life, there is an urgent need for consistency and order in the new family. The child, whether he is aware of it or not, pleads for a firm and reliable structure that he can count on and operate within.

After the honeymoon, Donny changed schools. He couldn't quite figure out what he was supposed to be doing, but since the teacher seemed cranky, he didn't want to ask her. He tried to be friendly to the kids, but they didn't seem to like him. He figured they already had their friends.

Donny missed the old neighborhood, the old house. When they'd moved out, he'd walked through the house saying goodbye. "Goodbye kitchen sink, goodbye back door, goodbye little bedroom," with the tears streaming down his face.

Now Mommy was always saying, "Do this for Uncle George, say that, kiss Uncle George goodnight." She kept him busy being one way or another with Uncle George. He figured if he did anything wrong with Uncle George, Mommy would get mad.

He couldn't understand why Uncle George needed him to kiss him; Mommy was always doing plenty of that. Then they'd go into their bedroom and close the door. Donny wasn't allowed to come in unless he knocked, and he had the feeling he wasn't supposed to knock. Donny felt closed out; he was by himself most of the time now.

One day he came home from school and told Mommy he wasn't going back. He told her he was going to go back and live in the old house and go to the old school where his friends were. He meant it too, but that night he and Uncle George played some catch in the backyard and pretty soon Uncle George had a bunch of the guys in the neighborhood all playing ball. Uncle George could bat one-handed and throw all sorts of crazy balls. The kids seemed to like him and Uncle George, and Donny decided to stick around a while and see what would happen.

GIVING GRIEF TO DAD'S NEW WIFE

When the father remarries the situation is different—unless, of course, he has custody. It's hard for the child to see his father's new home and realize that he doesn't live there, that it isn't his house. Sometimes the child finds that he doesn't really even have a room or even some space of his own in his father's house. Other children may be taking his place, living with his father, or later born into the new marriage. Often a child tests out his father's love by what one stepchild called "giving grief" to his stepmother. This behavior can include ignoring her, treating her like a servant, vying with her for Father's total attention, doing any number of things to her to see just whose side Dad is on.

Unfortunately, fathers often fall for this. Burdened with guilt, they allow too much, ignore bad manners, pretend it isn't happening—whatever "it" is. Feeling that they will be loved less if they discipline, fathers may sit by as the kids torment the stepmother into tears.

The child tests, and tests, and tests, sometimes bringing to pass the very things he fears. Or he behaves, and behaves, and behaves, fearful that any misdeed could bring his world to ruins around him. His very behavior may appear phony or mechanistic, and he may fail to win the family friends he's trying to win.

The child may be getting more, but the fear of loss and more loss seizes him at the beginning. He acts out the fear in one way or the other. The adults and the child in step must work together to dissolve this fear. Should it not dissolve, anger and hostility may be unwelcome guests in the household for years to come.

MISPERCEPTIONS AND MISPLACED ANGER

Children respond to any threat to their emotional security with fantastic anxieties, denials, distortions of reality, or displacement of feelings. And these reactions don't help the children to cope but rather put them at the mercy of events.

A child may direct his anger with Mom toward Stepmom, and multiply it a few times. He may load his fury with his father on his stepdad or on his stepmom. He may direct his hostility to his stepmother on stepbrothers or sisters. He may work it out in any number of ways, denying, distorting, refusing to see, and heaping all his negative feelings on the wrong people. These steppeople are not likely to lie down and accept the acting out without rancor, and the stepchild gets himself into a worse jam.

Much of the misplaced anger so common to step is based on the original breakup and the grievances and distortions surrounding that. A stepchild often unconsciously feels that he has to punish a stepparent—it's a way of getting even with the real parent. Consciously, he may never accept the fact that the breakup of the original family was inevitable.

What can a stepparent do? First, give the anger an opportunity to heal. Understanding its source, the stepparent can armor himself against hurt and possibly avoid responding in kind. Talking about it helps.

"You're not my father. I hate you."

"I hear you. We still have to live together. You are angry with me. You miss your dad? It must be hard. Are you angry with him?"

Sometimes the counterpart parent reinforces the misperceptions, encouraging the child to reject the stepparent. For example, a father sympathizes with his child over every dissatisfaction with the stepfather and the home, validating the child's wildest distortions. Or a mother runs down the stepmother, taking small truths and blowing them into exaggerated deficiencies (social drinker becomes alcoholic, and so on).

There is a great deal of brainwashing that goes on on both sides in step. Until a child is older, it is almost impossible for him to evaluate the propaganda. Sometimes he never does. Sometimes it works in reverse. Having heard enough bad-mouthing of both parents, children we have seen have screamed out in defiance that they will not listen to either parent. We have also seen children go live with the parent being blamed in order not to have to hear any more negative propaganda.

Idealization of one's parents creates problems for stepparents—implicitly, by comparison, they come up wanting. Somehow, the thinking goes, if Mom is good, Stepmom isn't so good. A stepparent who fights this with logical discussion gets nowhere. Besides, the child needs to believe in the goodness of his parent. But the goodness gets exaggerated, and sometimes it takes a saint to go along with the fiction. The best antidote is contact. The stepparent can arrange for his stepchild to have as many extended visits as possible with the biological parent.

Stepchildren have a dodge that they use. It goes like this: If you were my real parent, things would be different. You'd understand me. You wouldn't punish me so hard. You'd be nicer to me, and I'd be better. A child getting bad grades in school may say that Stepdad would understand if he were his real dad. The problem with the dodge is that it may prevent the child from taking responsibility for his part in the problem, and it may prevent the stepparent from helping.

Sometimes it isn't a dodge: the child is right. Things would be different if the stepparent were the real parent. After all, most stepparents don't initially have presumptions in the stepchild's favor. Stepparents do often use a stepchild as a scapegoat for their own troubles or deficiencies. Furthermore, stepparents frequently don't really want the child around.

Obviously, then, not all of a stepchild's step perceptions are distorted or exaggerated. Nor is all his anger and resentment misplaced. For many stepchildren, there are ample reasons for resentment. A stepchild is probably correct when he sees the stepparent as taking from him a good portion of his parent's time. He may be right when he feels shoved aside, no longer central to his parent's thinking. The love may well be diluted, the financial pie cut differently. Furthermore, the child may be right when he believes that somebody is talking about him and working against him behind his back. It's not surprising that stepchildren have fantasies of breaking up the marriage. They also have marvelously inventive fantasies of somehow getting rid of the stepbrothers and stepsisters or new children born into the marriage. The stepchild nourishes a romantic notion of either getting the parent to himself, or getting his own parents back together again, or both.

GETTING RID OF STEPPARENTS

Most children at some time in their lives have fantasies of getting rid of the rival same-sex parent and having the opposite-sex parent all to themselves. When a family breaks up, the child may be plagued by a sense of guilt that he indeed was the cause of the breakup. He may attempt to alleviate the guilt by endeavoring to destroy this marriage in order to bring his parents together again. As the stepparent is not his parent he now has a license to wreck this marriage in hopes of either restoring the original marriage or getting the parent to himself again.

Living in step provides fertile ground for fantasizing. Babies get flushed down toilets, infants in carriages get let go at the top of the hill with traffic coming, small children fall into the pool and drown. Plane crashes, car accidents, heart attacks, falling through the ice, eating a can of soup with botulism can take care of the older people. And then there's always divorce. The parent catches the stepparent doing something vicious to the stepchild, realizes how awful the stepparent is, and sends the stepparent packing, repenting to the child for putting him through so much agony. Positive creative disaster can also happen in the daydreams of step. Both parents can miraculously become free and remarry and live happily ever after, doting on the child. Or maybe they don't get back together again, but child and parent live happily together alone without the interference of that outsider.

Why not? Literature is rich with such fantasy fulfillment. Go ahead. Name one fairy tale in which the stepchild loses out in the end. It isn't even a matter of accommodation and learning to live together; the stepsibs and stepparents come to a dismal end.

Snow White ended up marrying a prince; but her stepmother, who had tried to destroy her, had to dance herself to death in red-hot iron shoes. Hansel and Gretel, after killing the witch and taking her fortune, came back to their father; while they were gone their stepmother had miraculously died. Cinderella married a prince. Graciously she provided a home for her stepsisters, who were blinded by birds at her wedding. Shortly after that they too died. All divinely disposed of.

Okay. Snow White and Hansel and Gretel and Cinderella are myths. The reality is a lot less extreme. Most of us would be dead or in jail if wishes came true. Stepmothers aren't that cruel, nor stepchildren that successful.

Not all stepchildren wish the marriage an ill end. Many work just as hard to make the marriage work. They've seen the first one crumble. They've experienced the lonely, lean times in between. They like living in the new family, and they try with all their resources to make the marriage continue smoothly.

Either way, they're bearing a burden. The success or the failure of the marriage is not the child's business. This feeling of omnipotence, of saving or destroying a parent's and stepparent's marriage, is a fantasy that needs to be squelched.

The couple can help by showing their strengths, their friendship, their affection, their durability. They are married, a unit. The child must realize that he does not have the power to drive a wedge into that love. Should you give the power to the child, you'll get the wedge.

BETWEEN HOMES

Coming home from a trip to California, fifteen-year-old Don gets off the plane wondering for a minute if somebody will be there. The plane was late, having circled for fifty minutes over Kennedy. He's feeling tired and queasy. Sort of depressed at being back in New York again, even though he missed his mother and George. There's nothing like a California beach. He always hates having to leave Dad.

He sees Mom and George, and the next thing he knows they're all over him. What about this? What about that? His hair, his jacket, his weight. Didn't Dad feed him regularly? What about Dad's girlfriends? Anyone special? What's the new house like? How many rooms? Dad's job? You'd think they were writing an article for *Penthouse* magazine or something.

He mentions that he and Dad played tennis every morning. George wants to know the scores. You can hear him calculating how good a tennis player Dad is.

Don gets it on both sides, transcontinentally—will they ever stop comparing? "Lay off!" he says, but they don't hear him. In the car he closes his eyes in an effort to catch some sleep and tune them out, but Mom keeps on.

Why is he so tired? He has circles under his eyes. What time did he go to bed out there? Don and Mom start arguing about his bedtime and curfew hour.

"Man oh man, do I hate to be back!" says Don. "You treat me like a stupid baby. At least Dad treats me like a human being."

"Human beings need sleep," says Mom.

"Sleep. That's all I get around here," says Don.

"Thanks for the appreciation," says George.

"For what? For keeping me from my father? I'd rather live with Dad!"

Soon everybody is talking at once. Mom is crying and George is really angry.

Don doesn't know whether to apologize or tell them to stop the car. At that moment George pulls the car over to the shoulder of the road and Don thinks for one horrified moment that he's going to tell him to get out. Then he hears George talking in a low, quiet voice; and somehow Don realizes that the crisis is almost over. Grudgingly he thinks, You've got to hand it to George. He's always there. . . .

Don's parents would be well advised to give him time in

which to reorient himself when he comes home. They should, as Don says, "lay off" for a while. Take it easy. Let him tell about his experiences when he's ready.

Should the child come home loaded with negative propaganda, it's best not to be drawn into the battle. Sometimes a simple "No, we don't see it that way" will suffice.

What about the child who comes home and says he wishes he were living with the other parent? Parents are hurt and upset. But, when a child says this, he may well be expressing the wish that he could live with both parents, or both sets of parents. Or he may simply be asking for clarification or assurance as to where home is. Or he could be expressing a fear that these very parents will send him to the other parent, or that both sets of parents may send him away. He may be asking for an affirmation of belonging.

Whatever the case, it's important for parent and stepparent to tell the child that the decision is not up to him, that his home is where his home is. Don's mother and stepfather, for example, could have told Don that they understood how much he missed his father, that it was only natural to wish sometimes that he could live with him. That the decision, however, was not up to Don. Don lived with them.

Visitation keeps alive the rivalry between the original parents. All too frequently, the stepchild is used as a judge or arbitrator between them. Keeping neutral may be his most difficult task. "You are," said one seasoned stepchild, "like a politician caught by a bunch of reporters. All you can honestly say is 'no comment.' "

One stepchild told us that one day she finally just had to become very firm with both parents. "I will not hear that kind of stuff about my father," she told her mother. "I will not hear that sort of talk about my mother," she told her father. "You're both wrong," she protested. It certainly didn't stop after her first protest, but eventually she "made them realize" the fact that she would not be suckered into their game any more.

The child would like to embrace both sets of parents without making value comparisons. Unfortunately, the comparisons are often forced upon him—and forced most openly at the times of transition from one family to the other, when he is least able to handle them. Don sensed the comparisons in his parents' questions, which fed his confusion and inspired his outburst.

Visitation also keeps alive the contact between the two parents. One of the major purposes of marriages is to create and raise children. This, then, is something that the couple is still doing together; in a sense, they are still married. The contact can be painful for parents, stepparents, and child.

For many stepchildren the shifting back and forth between homes, between parents, is the most difficult part of being a stepchild.

Each time the child goes back and forth he re-experiences in a small way the feelings surrounding the original breakup of the home, says Dr. Martha Leonard, associate professor of Clinical Pediatrics, Yale Child Study Center. The child feels some of the pain that went with it because the two parents he loves are not together any more. In addition, he may re-experience whatever resentment he might initially have had toward the stepparent who took the parent's place. In a sense the wound is not allowed to heal—each time it is reopened, sensitized.

It is particularly difficult for the child who has a good relationship with both parents. He loves both parents and wants to be both places.

No wonder, then, that parents and stepparents experience the turmoil of a child returning from a visit to the other parent. One way or another—by fighting, rebellion, sickness, insomnia, rudeness, withdrawal—he expresses the pain and conflict. The child's own pattern of defenses influences the style of acting out. Some may be quiet and withdrawn to the point of rudeness. Others may be angry and rebellious.

Unfortunately, the parents cannot make this transition easy, any more than they can smooth out all the bumps in life for the child. All they can do is try to understand what is happening—if the child picks a fight with his stepmother a half hour after he arrives, accept it for what it is. He's ill at ease and out of his usual equilibrium at this point.

With an older child, it is possible to talk about the problem, perhaps when he's getting ready to go off for the next visit. It may be that the child will help the parent, ease the transition. Even so, there is no escaping from the fact that these feelings will be aroused. There's also no denying the fact that understanding their source takes out a lot of the sting.

The question of a dominant home is one that comes up frequently when the children are in boarding schools and the visitation is shared between homes. Experts tell us that the child needs one place that he can call home. There must be one parent or set of parents that takes the dominant responsibility for the raising of the child. It does not augur well for the child to seesaw back and forth between two sets of separate but equal homes. This may result in the child's feeling that he basically has no home at all. We all need to know that we have a place where we belong—a place that we do not have to ask to come to, that we can come back to at any time.

GINNIE AND THE "CRUEL" STEPFATHER

GINNIE

I'm seventeen. My mother and father got divorced when I was twelve. I cried, but they had been fighting a lot. My mother remarried when I was thirteen. My father a year later. I have two sisters, one older, one younger.

When my about-to-be-stepfather first came around, I didn't like him much. But then, as I got to know him better, I really got to like Fred. When Mom told us she was getting married, we seemed so happy.

I didn't want to move away from my old home town and all my friends. I had no friends in the new place and didn't really try. I was so down. I hated the new school. All I could do was to wish it had never happened. Everything—the move to the new town and Mom's marrying Fred.

Finally I realized I wasn't getting anywhere fighting, and I decided to make friends. I began to be more friendly and enjoy myself. Also I started going to a private day school that I liked much better.

I was sort of curious about my stepbrothers and their friends, and I got along with my stepsisters pretty well. In fact, Sally and I are really close. My own sisters and I became closer because of them. Even my youngest sister, Pam, and I are getting over some of the fighting we used to do so much of.

I definitely resent my stepfather. I resent most of all his power and authority. For the past two years, Fred and I have been having a lot of fights. He's bringing me up. I never really had an authority figure who really laid down the rules.

STEPFATHER

Ginnie was really down, especially that first year. She walked around sad and depressed.

The public school she was in was overcrowded and run down. As her father showed no inclination to pay for the private school, I did it. I thought it would make her happy.

Her mother was relieved to see Ginnie go to another school.

We all try hard with Ginnie. She either seems to be boiling over in anger, or gazing off into space somewhere.

I walk into the room, but she doesn't acknowledge my presence. When I speak to her, she often looks right through me, like I'm not there.

Her glumness drags down the whole household. Often she'll do exactly what her mother has told her not to do. I can't sit by and watch this happen. She makes both Dori and me miserable at times.

GINNIE

All of a sudden it happened, and it was somebody else. It wasn't my dad. I feel, hey—wait a minute—who are you? Who are you to tell me what to do? I realize he does support me, and there are certain expectations of his that I should live up to, within reason. I believe that he also should compromise, bending my way. Which doesn't happen. I get good grades, I got a job, I work around the house, I take care of the younger sisters, I do everything that they ask.

But Fred still expects more. Like he lays down these rules, and he tells me what to do. I say—hey—give me some reasons. Like the rule that boys aren't allowed on the second floor is absurd. My room is the most comfortable place for me. When I'm comfortable, the people around me are comfortable. I don't have a boyfriend. And I'm not looking for that right now anyway. I do have friends who are boys. We like to go upstairs and talk. You can't even get your privacy for something as simple as talking . . .

We were on vacation at the beach. My father and his wife happened to be vacationing there too. Pam, my sister who's ten, was purposely annoying me, and it upset me. I tried to reason with her, and that didn't work. So I was going to try and shape her up—take her down to the beach and push her face in the water. As I was taking her out, she started screaming her head off.

Fred came out, and he grabbed my arms. The minute somebody grabs me forcefully, I just fly right off the handle. That's my fault. I should be able to control my temper, but obscenities just slip out when I'm upset. I called him a "fucking asshole." Well, he really got mad. He even slapped me a couple of times.

STEPFATHER

I will not be spoken to that way. She talks about communication. What she's always doing is walking away. The insult of turning her back on me, after all I do for her! I don't have to do what her father should be doing, but I want the best for her. It has all been going on for too long, much too long.

GINNIE

On the way home from the beach, the whole family went out to dinner. When the younger girls went to the ladies' room, I apologized to Fred. He didn't accept the apology. He said we'd discuss it when we got home.

We got home, he sat me down and started in right away—just as powerful as ever, saying, "I'm tired of playing games with you. I'm tired of all the shit I get from you. I'm going to lay down the rules now. You're not going to say a thing about them, and you are going to obey them, or get out."

They are always saying how there is a lack of communication. They don't even let me communicate with them. Or even ask questions. How the hell can they ever expect to get anything resolved? So I started to open my mouth and say, "Wait a minute—I can't listen to this!"

He got so angry, he came up and took me by the hair, and started hitting me. For about fifteen minutes he used physical force on me.

Well, if people have to stoop to that level, that they use to train an animal with, I just can't take it.

At times I would flare up. Then I would say to myself, "What are you doing, you're acting just like he is." I tried to stay peaceful and calm, but he was pulling my hair and twisting it. I just hadn't ever gone through anything like that before, and Mother wasn't doing anything to help.

He kicked me out. He packed my bags and threw me out the door. The whole thing was like an awful nightmare.

They said I could stay if I'd see a psychiatrist, but I don't believe I need a psychiatrist. Here's this guy sitting at this desk, and he thinks that in one hour a week he can take all your problems and absorb them. When there's a lack of communication, how can a third person solve it?

STEPFATHER

She hardly apologized to me. Besides, apologies aren't enough at this point. She wasn't going to walk away from me this time. She was either going to go to a psychiatrist or leave. There are seven children merged into this family. There are bound to be problems. We prepared for them: both Dori and I have talked a lot with a psychiatrist, and many of the children have seen him, and we've gone with them. Ginnie refused to see him.

Her father was nearby for a change. Her mother and her

father and I had been talking about her father taking her. He refused.

For months she had been blatantly doing things we forbid—smoking marijuana in her room, in this house, going away for weekends when we forbade it.

Her father, when he does it, contributes $150 a month to her support, all her clothes, her summer activities, etc., etc. . . . and what do I get in return? "You fucking asshole."

GINNIE

I went to live with some friends for a week, a very "together" family.

Fred pulled me out of school for a couple of days, but it wasn't very successful. I still went to my classes. He wanted to show me how much power he had. He really does.

A teacher I like and have known for a couple of years went and told them my side, saying I was wrong, but I would apologize. What they did was make a mountain out of a molehill. They could have let it go nice and easy, but they extracted promises and conditions. Mother and Fred are both pragmatic, and Fred has his values.

The next day I came to school, and the teacher told me what they'd said. I went home that night, and they were very nice to me, and it does seem as if things will go all right. One thing I know is that I'm never going to call him a fucking asshole again. It's a matter of eating humble pie for a while.

When the marriage was new, I was very unhappy. I didn't consider it home. I didn't look forward to anything. I wished it had never happened. It was something I had to realize myself.

What would I tell an about-to-be-stepchild? I would say that it will be rough at first, but it's going to be the best experience that ever happened to you. That you are going to realize a lot of things about people. Looking at it now, this new marriage is really a good experience, despite the hassle we've had. You lose something, but you gain something else, and you learn to grow with it and expand.

FATHER

We had spent the day together. All day in the sun and sand. The two girls, Ginnie and Pam, seemed to be 100 percent better with each other. Ginnie actually seemed to be mothering Pam rather than fighting with her.

Problems, problems are all her mother talks about. Dori always wants me to get together with Fred, when she's not taking me to court for more money. Money is all she thinks about.

My girls are wonderful. And they love their Daddy. There is nothing wrong with them. They're normal, healthy girls. That day they were angels. Ginnie now seems to be getting along with my new wife better. They, all three girls, were adorable and charming to be with.

Ginnie is developing into some young woman! I'd love to have her live with us, but it's impossible with my schedule.

MOTHER

I cried my eyes out when Fred went up there and dragged out a suitcase and made her pack her bags. We gave her the chance. She could have elected to see the psychiatrist. She holds to her father's notions about psychiatrists—that they are somehow judgmental and are going to find some deep awful secret or that they just can't piece things together in a few minutes every week. We try to tell her, of course they can't, but perhaps he would be of some help. She won't listen. She's just like her father. He made jokes all the way through our attempt to salvage our marriage with the help of a psychiatrist.

I had to let Fred throw her out. He does so much for her. She will hardly say thank you, much less even be polite to him. That kind of man just won't take that kind of language. My heart breaks for the child.

I wish her father would take her, just to see what it's like. But he won't. He never stays in one place long enough.

STEPMOTHER

Dori called at eleven at night. Her voice was tense. Her husband had kicked Ginnie out of the house and is refusing to pay her tuition and withdrawing her from school. She asked if we would keep an eye out for Ginnie as she thought she might show up at our house. I said, "Of course." But her father wasn't there: he had left that morning for a business trip to Europe. Of course she could stay. I would leave her a note, and the door would be open for her.

My God, what had happened?

We'd just had such a wonderful day with them. I was thinking about calling to say what a wonderful job she and Fred were doing with the children—how changed they were from last year when Ginnie seemed so depressed and down. How well they were getting along. What a delightful day we had had together.

I can't believe it. What did the child do? . . . "A fucking asshole." Sounds just like her father.

Dori said Ginnie and her stepfather argue constantly, that she and Ginnie couldn't get along. She asked if we would take Ginnie to live with us for a year.

I said no, I didn't think it was the best thing, all the way around. Her father, the way he is, and not enough money to do it. I thought it would be better if Ginnie worked things through with her stepfather.

THERAPIST, Nancy Winston, M.S.W.

Ginnie's mother and father divorced when she was reaching the stage of adolescence. In adolescence oedipal feeling recurs—the daughter has unconscious sexual feelings toward the father. In the ideal intact family the daughter is allowed to work through these feelings. She desires attention from the father. She gets the attention. She also receives reassurance that the father loves her, but not in a sexual way. She grows to understand that her love for her father is okay, and that her own sexuality is okay. Her self-esteem, having been assaulted by one more rocky period of childhood, is once again intact.

Ginnie sees her father irregularly. As with all children of divorce, there exist unconscious feelings of being left by him. She is never really assured of her father's love, although, when they are together, she feels that he loves her. But she never quite knows when the next time they'll be together will come.

She openly resents her stepfather. He is in the place and doing the things that she feels her father should. Although Ginnie credits her stepfather with materially caring for her, she feels that any recognition of loyalty to him would be a recognition of disloyalty to her father. If she did recognize her loyalty to Fred, she would have to recognize emotionally that her father was not there for her and that her stepfather was indeed fulfilling the major part of the fatherly role now.

Ginnie cannot give any loyalty to her stepfather because the relationship with her father is so irregular that all her energies must be directed toward confirming the fact that her father loves her. Should she acknowledge the fathering and caring that her stepfather does for her, it would weigh too heavily on the slender thread of her father's and her love.

If she were sure of the love of her father, then she would in time be open and able to give and receive love from her stepfather.

Basically our self-esteem hooks up to our feelings about our parents, especially during the crucial period of adolescence when self-esteem is being re-evaluated in terms of parents and peers.

In addition Ginnie may have undealt-with anger toward her mother for the loss of her father. Should she express this, she fears, she would lose her one remaining accessible parent.

So Fred, the stepfather, the alien, the newcomer, is the perfect target for these pent-up hostile emotions. She uses him as a viable excuse for her resentments, an object for her hostility. She is not putting this on Fred as a person, but on Fred as the symbol of the absent father.

Her loss of her father was never really mourned. In a divorce situation, the child is not able to mourn the loss—the person is still in the picture. But loss of family could and should be mourned. It seldom is in divorce.

From appearances the period was too short between divorce and remarriage. Ginnie never had a chance to incorporate her feelings for her father back into herself. When we love someone, we put energy from ourself into that person. Love is energy. When we mourn, we go over and over again everything about that person. By mourning that loss, we're able to incorporate energy of the lost relationship back into ourselves.

After a death, children can mourn their loss fully and come out feeling able to carry on and eventually have another fulfilling relationship. In divorce, children are often discouraged from mourning the loss of the family. There has been no death. The parent is still alive. The child is often propelled into a hopeless quest of reunion with the absent parent. Then, in the remarriage, the stepperson is often seen as the hindrance to ever getting the lost parent back.

Despite all that her stepfather felt he did for her, Ginnie continued not to acknowledge his presence or his parental authority. A powerful man felt powerless. Seeing her father at the beach when she had not seen him for many months stirred up all Ginnie's longing for him. That, in turn, re-emphasized all the negative feelings toward Fred.

Fred finally had to give in to his feelings of anger and powerlessness by asserting his authority over material things—withdrawing her from the school she liked and throwing her out of the house.

His pain or anger or discontent had no effect upon her because she wouldn't allow herself an emotional investment in him. She didn't care if he was displeased with her. He had to do what he did to have an impact on her.

I get the feeling that Ginnie feels alone in life. Her mother has Fred. They seem to her to be a unit which shuts her out. Her father has his wife. One of her sisters is too old to feel this and the other is too young. So she has a feeling of powerlessness.

The family had been talking about Ginnie's going to live with her father. Her father said this would be impossible. So, having the incident with Pam in the presence of Fred, with her father nearby for the first time in months, Ginnie had an excellent opportunity to test—through bad behavior. Where did she belong? Who cared, and how much? Since her father was around, she could test him to see if he would take her now that she was really in need.

Knowing that she always had a place, that her mother would never really kick her out, Ginnie proceeded to act against her stepfather. One also has the hunch that this whole transaction gave her the excuse to listen to her stepfather and to be on better terms with him.

From the dialogue we have here, we see that Ginnie worked it out in the terms that were best for her—"deal with Fred, eat humble pie"—and laugh.

She refused to see the psychiatrist; however, she chose to spend some of these nights away from home with a couple actively working in Gestalt therapy. She compromised. She compromised with Fred. She is beginning to respect his authority; she is realizing her role in this family; she has solved many of her problems. She learned from her experience and is beginning to have some insight into what her role was in this family incident, and to apply that knowledge to future interactions.

There may well be future incidents that are angry, dramatic, unpleasant. But the incident at the beach and afterward ended up as a growth experience for Ginnie.

7

Interaction

THE SCENE DOESN'T start clean. To the stepparent, his spouse's children are the living symbols and products of an alien union and at the same time the offspring of a loved one. To the children, it feels as though the stepparent is masquerading as somebody he isn't—an impostor claiming a position that belongs to their other parent. Built into the very structure of step is an emotional conflict of interest.

Ambivalent and negative feelings are a reality of living in step. The stepperson may feel: I like you and I dislike you; I want you here and I can't stand you here; I want you to succeed and I want you to fail. Or perhaps the stepperson's feelings are predominantly negative. Disliking a family member is ugly, particularly when that member is a child. Disliking a parent or stepparent is dangerous: you could get in a lot of trouble—might even get thrown out. Thus the unpretty feelings become obscured, cut off from direct expression. They aren't acceptable.

Sometimes the facts get concealed as well. An extreme case was presented to us by a grown stepchild who told us that she had not known for the first twelve years of her life that her father was really her stepfather. Her step paternal grandparents raised her and her half brother. The brother was clearly preferred. What must I do to make them like me? she kept asking herself. She would try, and try, and try; but still it wasn't enough. Her parents had tried to protect her from the truth—which would have been kinder. The trouble was in the situation, but she assumed the trouble was in herself.

MYSTIFYING THE CHILD

Children are often not given information that they can use about what is happening in the family, what the situation is, where the other parent has gone, and why. They try to find out the facts, and if they can't they make them up.

According to San Francisco family therapist Warde Laidman, it is always better to tell the truth, even when there appears to be a rejection on the part of one of the parents. "The hard thing," he says, "is to get parents to come to terms with the facts—to say, for example, that they reject the child. Sometimes they can't admit it, and so they give mixed messages: you need your father, need exposure to the theater, better to live in the country, and so on. Most kids can cope with the rejection, but you can't kid them. It's the mystification, the mysterious, the unpredictability of responses that is so injurious."

There's a lot of kicking the dirt over the tracks, over the facts, over the emotions, in step. Concealing this, concealing that, putting the masks on, and pretending that what happened didn't happen, what is going on isn't going on. Often an open person marries into a closed family and gets trapped into the system. Always the lies are for the sake of the child. Nonsense. Haul out the skeletons and let them dance around. Maybe then they'll go away. They can't get away if you keep them locked up.

Mystification about the past as well as the present happens all too frequently in step. In one stepfamily that had come for counseling the problem was a boy who was bright but had problems in learning. Gerda Schulman, a New York psychiatric social worker, tried to elicit facts about the mother's former marriage to the father of the boy. The mother became hysterical: it was something she could not speak about without tremendous upset.

The mother said that she had told the boy a number of times, "If you have any questions about Daddy or the divorce, ask me." But his response, she said, had always been, "I'm not interested. I don't care."

On the one level, the verbal level, the mother's message was "Ask me if you have any questions." On the nonverbal level, her message was "Don't ask me, we don't discuss it"; for whenever anybody mentioned her ex-husband she would cry. She was giving the child a mixed message.

The therapist connected his learning problem with the "don't ask" message. Preventing him from being inquisitive about himself and his past affected other areas: I'm not interested. I don't want to know. It doesn't matter.

DOUBLE MESSAGES

People in step are *especially subject to giving and receiving double messages.* A stepmother says her stepson can set up his trains in the living room, but she doesn't like having them there, and she shows it. Her acceptance is false. The child knows how she feels—no matter what she says. He's being given contradictory cues: do it and don't do it. He wants to set up the trains, but he wants to be liked by his stepmother. What should he do?

The problem here is that the child reads the stepmother's rejection of the behavior as a rejection of himself. Much better if the stepmother could simply say, "Not in the living room."

A stepmother may say to her stepchildren, "Come as often as you can. We love to have you here. The door is always open." Then, when they do come, she shows nonverbally that they aren't all that welcome.

By not honestly facing her own feelings about the children and telling her husband the truth—that she doesn't want them around so much—she is failing to take responsibility for her rejections. To her it isn't right not to make the children totally welcome at all times in their father's house. And yet, of course, she doesn't.

The children get the signals and begin to stay away, but the words keep coming. "We want you to visit. We miss you. Don't you care about us?" Either way the children are wrong, damned if they do and damned if they don't.

Sometimes conflicting messages get piped in from different sources. A stepfather says *this* is the way we do it. The mother says *that* is the way we do it. Or father says, "Respect your mother." Stepmother shows the children a thousand reasons why they can't.

Sometimes a child receives conflicting ethical commands from the two sides of the family. The mother and stepfather are teetotalers. The instruction is "Don't drink." The father and stepmother are tipplers. The message is "Eat, drink, and be merry." Or the stepmother promotes scrupulous honesty while the mother has the children lying about their ages at movie theaters and airports.

Mixed messages can lead to confusion in the child's mind. So too can a message that isn't mixed but is simply untrue. A child is told to go to bed at seven because he is tired. "I'm not tired." "Yes, you are." Can the child trust his own perceptions? Actually, his mother and stepfather want to be alone for a while before they go to bed. Why can't they just say so and let the child watch TV, play, or look at books in his room?

Mother and Stepdad both say that Stepdad loves little Johnny just as much as if he were his own son. But Stepdad is continually giving out signals that Johnny's presence irritates him.

Johnny says to his mother, "What does Stepdad have against me?"

Now a well-meaning mother who wants her son to feel as though he belongs, as though he is loved, might respond, "Why, nothing, Johnny. You know Stepdad loves you a lot."

At this point Johnny is being told that he isn't really picking up what he is picking up. He's being told not to trust his perceptions.

An equally well-meaning mother who is receiving the same negative signals as Johnny might say, "Johnny, I don't know. Sometimes it's hard for a stepfather to feel loving when a little boy is busy being all the things that little boys are. Sometimes the busyness can be irritating. Why don't we talk to him about it?"

Thus she supports the child in his perceptions, indicates that the trouble might lie in the situation rather than in the child himself, and leads the way for open discussion—and, perhaps, an alteration of both stepfather's and child's behavior. A much better outcome than false assurances like the following are likely to bring about:

"How can you think such a thing! Of course you don't hate baby brother!" (She's been jealous of him since the day he was born.)

"Of course your father loves you!" (He's been around twice in the past three years.)

"Stepmother is so good to you." (Like hell she is.)

"Your stepbrothers really like you a lot." (They've never been anything but mean.)

"Stepgrandparents like you so much." (In five years, they never bothered to send a birthday or Christmas present.)

These children are receiving messages that contradict their thoughts, emotions, or perceptions. The messages to the child are all too clear: you can't rely on your thinking process, you can't be sure of your emotions (you aren't feeling what you are feeling), you can't make an accurate judgment about what's going on around you. Conveyed consistently, messages like these "help" a child lose his checks on reality. Which, of course, puts him in serious trouble with himself.

"DON'T EXIST" AND OTHER PUT-DOWNS

Hand in hand with mixed messages goes a lot of direct and indirect discounting of the person in general. The stepfamily is, in fact, a fertile place for the manufacture of discounts. Feelings of don't be, don't exist, don't hassle me, go away, you don't belong, filter through the blended family and fester within it.

We all know the scenarios:

The child bounds into the room. "I just made junior varsity hockey! I'm going to play . . ."

The stepparent says, "Your shoes are dirty. You're getting mud on the rug."

Or the child is halfway through an exciting story, and the stepparent starts discussing something else with someone else.

Similar putdowns occur at times in all families. In step they can be more frequent and more extreme.

Stepfather and stepchild go fishing. Stepchild gets a fish. "Ooohh, it's a big one! It's hard to hold!"

A nurturing parent says, "Hang on there! Hold the tip up!

You're getting him." Or, "Oh, well, you'll get the next one." The message is: "You can do."

A discounting parent says, "You're not doing it right. You've got the tip down again. You're not reeling in fast enough. You're going to lose it! Here, give it to me." The message is: "You can't do."

Stepchildren do it too. Their discounts can come across verbally, in implied putdown or out-and-out insult; or nonverbally, by a gesture of annoyance when the stepperson walks into the room, or by a tone of voice.

For a hard-working stepparent struggling to help raise another person's child or children, few things can seem crueler or more unjust than the discounts of a stepchild. And yet, considering the stepchild's developing psyche, the discounts of a stepparent or older stepsibling are more injurious.

The child doesn't yet know who he is; the adult's self-image has pretty much been built. The child is still building his self-concept; what happens to him now may well be with him forever. Stepsiblings or stepparents who discount can lead him to self-fulfilling conclusions about himself. Gee, I really am stupid. Nothing I ever do turns out right. Nobody likes me. And so forth.

The stepchild is the one least equipped to know what's going on, or how to handle what's happening. The burden of recognizing and dealing with the discount therefore lies with the adults.

The game can be played in anger or hurt. The putdowns can be tit for tat, straight on, or behind the back. In any case, discounter and discountee are playing a destructive game.

The damaging factor in most discounts is that they're not direct. They're ulterior, borderline, left-handed, suggested. If they *were* direct, they could be better dealt with. The indirect discount is an undertone: it's what the kids call vibrations. It's more dangerous. You don't "get it," you just get a kind of feeling about yourself.

The problem, then, becomes one of bringing discounts into the open, of dealing squarely with something that is by nature oblique. When a stepchild is rude, the stepparent or parent could simply own up to his feelings. "Hey, Sam, it makes me feel bad, like I'm not important, when you act like that."

Some people are by their very nature nurturing; others are discounting. When a nurturing person from a nurturing family marries into a discounting family, the scene can be painful, especially where children who have been accustomed to nurturing are involved.

One has to recognize the discount and defuse it. The secret lies in hearing what is actually being said, verbally or nonverbally, and understanding from what emotional (not rational) place it's coming.

Understanding, of course, rarely suffices. Something needs to be done about the problems. The frustration in dealing with discounts lies in the fact that the discounter will usually deny. ("What do you mean? I tell them again and again how much we want them here." Or "I did too say hello." Or "I certainly did *not* look at you like that.") The discounter should be made aware that the discountee has seen it, felt it, doesn't like it, and will react to it.

THE "I FEEL . . ." SYSTEM

Some stepfamilies have adopted the "I Feel" system as a way of owning up to discounting and of clarifying other troublesome areas. By prefacing a statement with "I feel," one can say almost anything. Each member of the family owns his own feelings and expresses them. Feelings are not good or bad—they simply are. And, if they are there, better to have them out in the open than festering somewhere below. *All* "I Feel" dialogue is acceptable.

Stepchild to stepfather. "I feel that you're spending too many weekends alone, away with my mother."

Stepfather: "You're lonely when we're gone? Or do you miss your mother?" (He waits for the child's response.)

Stepchild: "Both! And I feel I want us to be more like a family—you know, a regular family with Mom and Pop and Buddy and Sis."

Stepfather: "You want us all to spend more time together."

Stepchild: "Yes. Do things like families do."

The feelings are out; the stepfather and mother and family can make some decisions around them. Even if the couple continues to go on the weekends alone, the child feels better for having spoken out and been heard. Perhaps some special weekend including the child can be planned and looked forward to.

Perhaps the couple hardly ever gets away alone together. That is not the point. The couple hears what the child is feeling, whether justified or not. One of the assets of the "I Feel" system is that you don't get into a battle over the facts and thereby immediately cut off expression.

Allowing the children complete expression about matters in no way surrenders the decision-making authority. What is permitted or done and what is talked about are two different matters. But, when parents understand the feelings surrounding something, they are more likely to make the correct decision.

Rule setting and expression of feelings can work together. Suppose the child says straight out, "I don't have to do what you say. You're not my mother."

Gerda Schulman suggests the following way of handling this. First, the stepparent goes to the natural parent and asks for support. And then the parent, in this case the father, goes to the child. "She is not your mother. She is not going to take your mother's place in terms of loving, but in terms of rule making, she and I are the ones who make the rules here."

The stepmother, then, could sit down with the child and explain. She could say, "I feel that every time I make a rule you compare me with Mommy. I know you are missing Mommy, but comparing me to her makes me feel angry, makes me feel hurt, and I get very grouchy, and that's not good for you. I get jealous . . . like you do with baby brother."

The stepmother is saying, "Help me, I'm human." Through further "I Feel" dialogue, she can help the child bring into the open his feelings about not wanting a stepmother in the house. She can make it clear that she is there permanently, nonetheless. The child does not have to love her—but come on, give her a break.

The couple can effectively use "I Feel" dialogue between themselves. A husband can say to his wife, "I feel I don't want your kids around so much. They really bother me. I feel that what they do to the house is nothing short of major housewrecking. I feel that we have just got to find a way to enjoy our home together without all this."

Dialogue like this leaves room for the couple to work something out. Of course, the mother can't send the children out to sea forever; but some rules could be set up about indoor behavior, some outside activities arranged. Perhaps the basement could be made into a soundproof family room. Something.

To ensure the effective working of the "I Feel" system, the family members have to be open to receiving the communication. They have to be wary of cutting it off at the inception with their own "I Feel" onslaught. In short, they have to listen.

Stepchild to stepmother: "I feel that you're taking all my father's money. I feel it belongs to Mom and us kids. We don't even have enough to have decent meals, and look where you're living."

Stepmother: "You feel you're short-changed."

Stepchild: "Right. I feel Dad just walked out and abandoned us."

Stepmother: "You wish your father had never left?"

Stepchild: "Sure. We used to be so happy together. I mean, they'd fight a little, but they didn't really mean it. Things were really nice—you know, the atmosphere. Everything was nice and easy. Mom was happy. We all were. And now here you are. And there we are. And Mom's so unhappy, and she works so hard, and we can barely get it together. It just isn't right. And sometimes it makes me so mad I can't even sleep. Sometimes I think I hate you and Dad!"

Stepmother: "You feel that Dad and I are causing your mother's unhappiness and troubles?"

Stepchild: "Right. Well . . . maybe sometimes she spends too much money on the wrong things. . . ."

Stepmother: "You think maybe she doesn't spend it all on running the household and on you kids."

Stepchild: "I know she doesn't. And sometimes she's so busy with her dates we never see her."

Stepmother: "You wish she'd stay home more."

Stepchild: "Yes. And I wish she'd shut up about Dad. She's always . . . Still, it isn't fair that you and Dad have everything, and we have nothing."

By suspending her own "I Feel," the stepmother was able to discover the true stretch of the child's feelings. The child was able to take a look at things and get rid of some of his bottled-up feelings. By telling it straight out to the stepmother, he was at least partially relieved of the necessity of showing his hostility through devious means. This lays a path for friendliness. The child begins to solve for himself some of the problems. Also, when the stepmother does talk (and this one probably will), the child will be more willing to listen to her side.

Had the stepmother exercised her own "I Feel" prerogative immediately rather than listening through the child's, it might have gone like this:

Stepchild: "I feel that you are taking all my father's money. I feel it belongs to Mom and us kids."

Stepmother: "Well, I feel that I am your father's wife, not she. And I feel that I work hard and contribute to the operation of this house. I pay for a lot of what costs us money around here. In fact, I get angry because your father pays so much money to your mother and you kids and nobody is very grateful."

Stepchild: "Well, hell, there's nothing to be grateful for. I feel it's unfair for you guys to live like this when we can barely make it."

Stepmother: "I feel that you can barely make it because of what your mother does with the money."

Stepchild: "I feel you don't know what you're talking about. My mother . . ."

This "I Feel" was used as a means to battle. Still, that's preferable to not getting feelings into the open. When combined with listening, "I Feel" can be useful indeed. Getting out feelings often seems to help them disappear like magic. And, then, feelings expressed aren't permanent. Hate expressed can make room for love.

8

Growing Up in Step

In the stepfamily one often finds a child who rarely misbehaves. The too-good child is the too-adapted child, the child who tries to do everything his parents expect of him.

The child may feel that his acts could be responsible for the making or the breaking of this marriage. The parent has impeded the natural behavior of the child with the message that, if he's bad, the terrible loss in the prior divorce could occur again. Or he may fear being cast away out of the stepfamily or losing the love of the remaining biological parent.

Some stepchildren spend their entire lives, at five or fifty, being the good little girl or boy. While this creates few troubles for the parents, the internal pressures on the child can be enormous.

The overly good child is holding in his anger, holding in his fear. To the parents, the child seems to need no special attention or help. The child's holding back, however, may result in his being carefully manipulative—not natural or spontaneous—or it may come out as a psychological or psychosomatic disorder —insomnia, constipation, headaches, sickness. Often behind the sickness is the fear of being cast away. (How can you send away a sick child?)

It can start with the divorce. "Children in a divorce situation generally are fearful of expressing anger," says Dr. Richard Gardner. "At the first, the child is angry because the parents are splitting. He's angry at his father—let's say the father is the one who's left the house. He sees the father as an abandoner, even though the mother may have thrown him out. He's afraid to to express anger at his mother because, now that Father has left the house, he has to be careful with her. She too could leave.

"So the situation is one which tends more to bring about the repression of anger than the acting-out of anger, though that certainly does happen. Often the acting-out is outside the home, with teachers, and friends."

In step, the too-good child may be being good to get what he wants. If he doesn't get it, he may explode. Often, his feelings come out explosively away from the home, while at home the child is still being too carefully good.

The too-good child needs to know that the family will continue regardless of what he does. That it is all right to be himself, that he will be loved regardless. Of course there will be requests and punishments, but the basic love will be surely there all the time.

CREATING THE TOO-GOOD CHILD

Christie describes how it was for her:

"I have a friend who has a normal family, a really good family. She can go home and be relaxed. She doesn't even know what family tension is. I think she maybe has one fight a week with her sister. I wish mine had been like that.

"I was nine when my mother remarried. Right from the start I've always tried. Mommy was always making such an effort, and I was always making such an effort. I think that was kind of assumed.

"I would get hurt, and just like a dumb bunny, I would come back and come back. They counted on my coming back. Just recently now, I'm tired of it, so I haven't been doing it. Mommy's tired of it too.

"I wish when I was younger someone had explained to me what was happening. Up until this year I haven't realized why I felt so insecure, why all of a sudden I would burst out crying in the middle of my piano lesson or something like that. I was feeling it, yet none of my friends were. I would probe them at lunch—don't you ever feel this way? Or that way?

"It's just like—you couldn't study. Or this underlying tension in your stomach.

"And sometimes I would just do a lot of crying. Why am I crying? Just now I'm understanding it's because there isn't that basic solid stability behind you.

"I have always felt that I should try and try and try. And I felt it was bad if I was angry with Dave, my stepfather. I've never expressed direct anger at Dave because he's always saying calm down, keep it in. He has these hand gestures starting at the top and bringing the palms down, keep it in, calm down.

"Anger's healthy. I heard that. Two boys are angry and wrestling and then they're off to the soda shop.

"Well, for me the tension's always there until I get with my friends and get to laughing and rolling on the ground. I can draw this little orange circle in my stomach where the tension is. I guess it's compression—yeah, repression.

"I don't think in a natural family they even think about it. I think with Mom and me, there was a before Daddy and an after Daddy. Before Daddy died, I can't really remember, but there was an atmosphere—it was just warm and easy and friendly, nothing specific, just a feeling. Now in the stepfamily, it becomes a constant question. And you're asked to be true to something outside yourself instead of yourself.

"I hope Mommy and Dave stay together because I think they really enjoy each other and get a lot from each other. I wouldn't want Mommy to be all alone when I'm away at college, and I would feel guilty like I ought to stay home with her. One thing I wish is that none of this had ever happened. It's been a bad dream."

Christie, from the beginning, was involved in keeping the family together. Her behavior and attitudes paralleled those of her mother. Her mother made efforts; so did Christie. Her mother became dissatisfied with her stepfather; Christie did too. Somehow she didn't feel free to relax and develop her own separate and independent relationship with her stepfather.

The tension that Christie feels is present in many stepfamilies. Something feels fragile, and everyone is being extra careful not to let "it" get broken. The insecurity of the husband or wife filters down. A muffled panic—"don't let this marriage fail"—is communicated.

Sometimes the child gets a message that he doesn't belong, that he'd better behave or he won't be around. Either the parent or the stepparent or both are encouraging the child to hold his feelings in. Don't. Don't. Don't. That's the message; the child gets it and doesn't, doesn't, doesn't.

The solution starts with the couple. If their relationship is trusting, relaxed, and accepting, they can engender the same feelings in the kids. If they can somehow work out their own insecurities together, they will be in a better position to create an atmosphere of ease and friendliness where children are permitted to be what they appropriately are at their particular age or stage in life. And permitted to talk about their feelings.

Frequently children in step are required to grow up too fast, to take responsibility too soon, to behave as adults when they're only children. Again, appropriate childlike behavior needs to be encouraged. Somehow the child needs to know that it (the family) is okay, and he's okay.

YOU DON'T HAVE TO LOVE HIM

The too-good child isn't much fun to himself or anybody else in the family. One mother tells how she helped her young daughter:

"Carol was, from the beginning of the remarriage, a dutiful stepdaughter, aiming hard toward perfection. All her gestures, all her talk, were designed and strained when her stepfather was there. One night, when I was tucking her in bed, I said, 'What do you think of Paul?' 'I love him, and I love you.' 'Look,' I said, 'you don't have to love him. You don't even have to like him. You have a father, and you always will. Paul can be your friend if you want. But even that's not necessary. All I ask is that you continue to be respectful because he's my husband and your stepfather.'

"From that day on, Carol became increasingly spontaneous

with Paul, and there's something irresistible about spontaneity. The two of them developed their own relationship, their own way of looking at things, their own sense of fun. Sometimes it completely escapes me, but they're having a good time."

THE TOO-BAD CHILD

Not all stepchildren, of course, are too good. Many are described, by the stepparents at least, as "too bad." In these children there's perpetual anger, hostility, surliness, sullenness, or rudeness—perhaps even delinquent behavior.

The child tests—to see if he will be kicked out, to see if anybody cares enough to stop him. Sometimes his behavior is a plea for recognition, for attention, for love. He often feels that somebody else is getting the love or attention that he wants.

A lot of stealing can go on in stepfamilies, along with a lot of lying. Stealing and lying go hand in hand, and one sees the behavior in children who feel abandoned or neglected or unhappy, who feel there isn't enough warmth around them. The way such a child gets his own love is by taking things rather than asking for them.

One father refused to face the fact that his daughter was stealing. His wife, the girl's stepmother, kept telling him that Betty was stealing things from their house. They'd show up at her mother's house. Things from the mother's house would show up at their house. A sort of transplanting of objects. But the father kept making excuses or explanations for it. Then one day the local police called him. Betty had been caught shoplifting in a drugstore. He had to admit the facts. They talked, he disciplined, she cried. They talked, she admitted to a pattern of stealing. They talked, they both cried, they became close. The discipline was carried out; she hasn't stolen since. She finally got the affirmation and the attention she needed.

IS PROFESSIONAL HELP INDICATED?

What are the danger signals, the signs that a child is in trouble and needs some help?

Dr. Lenore Terr, a San Francisco child psychiatrist, warns parents and stepparents to watch for changes or problems in basic body functions—eating, eliminating, or sleeping.

Perhaps a child refuses to eat, and a stepparent attempts to force the eating. Or it may be the reverse. A stepchild may feel that the best food—the biggest piece of cake, the juiciest piece of meat—goes to the natural child, or at any rate not to himself. Dr. Terr told of an adult patient who has eating disorders that go back to an actual challenge from the stepmother who gave the best food to her own child.

Some children who are three, four, and five years old take revenge on the stepparent by having bowel movements on the floor, spreading feces on the wall, and so on. The only weapon a very young child may have is excrement.

A stepmother can talk with a child, can show him that she understands his loss, his resentment, the fact that she has come into his life and he doesn't understand. A preventive visit or two to a child psychiatrist may be in order if the behavior persists.

An angry seven-, eight-, or nine-year-old may start wetting his bed. The child doesn't know why he does it. The parent should be aware that this behavior may be unconscious, unwitting, but still hostile.

Dr. Terr advises talking about the problem: "Look, I know you're angry and don't want me in your house, but you can just come right out and say it—you don't have to wet the bed. I'm not moving out because you want me to, but I understand how you feel. I might feel the same in your position." The stepmother might add, "You're not making it easier for me either. Your behavior is not making it any easier for your father and me. Sometimes I resent it."

If a child is having trouble sleeping, is sleepwalking, or comes frequently into the parents' room at night, this too is a danger sign.

Is a child becoming overly seductive? Spending a great deal of time in masturbating? Whatever the behavior, don't come down heavily on the child. Figure out how to approach the problem, or try a session or two with a psychiatrist. Two, three, or four sessions may take care of it.

There may be actual psychiatric symptoms: learning disturbances, failure in school the year the parents remarry, sudden difficulty in making or getting along with friends, lying, cheating, stealing.

Often the depth of disturbance goes unrecognized. The parent and stepparent may feel that all the child needs is love and attention, or worse, that the child can't be helped and is just bad or dumb. The child must be dealt with, for the emotional disturbance of any one person can permeate the entire family.

Another danger signal in a child is the absence of change or progress. Dr. John Leanard, a California child psychiatrist, sees this as critical. No matter how troubled the situation is, if there is any resolution taking place, he is inclined to let the situation ride. He is more concerned where behavior is stuck, unyielding, unchanging.

What new parents need to understand, Dr. Leonard says, is that often in step they are in a situation that can't be undone by good parenting. The stepparent and the biological parent with custody often get themselves into a horrible bind trying to do something that can't be done from within the family. Good parenting is helpful, but work with the child at times has to be done by an outsider. Sometimes the task of correcting the problems shouldn't be undertaken by the parents. Expert professional help may be the best move possible.

SIBLINGS

In the intact family, sibling rivalry is taken for granted and dealt with as best one can. In the stepfamily, particularly in the beginning, sibling rivalry is, very often, exaggerated.

The child suddenly has competitors for his parent's love and for his old place in the family. They come not only in ones, but twos, threes, sometimes sixes. And they bring with them an adult competitor, the parent's new spouse, the stepsibling's certain ally.

It's not only place and parent that are threatened but possessions as well. The other kids may take them, break them, or simply get new things that the child thinks he deserves. We have seen Christmas in stepfamilies where children hardly noticed their gifts for looking to see what the "others" got. Some stepchildren keep tallies of the comparative values of birthday and Christmas presents. One stepchild reported that his stepmother got a fur coat while he got a Tonka truck. Where a child seems worried about gifts and possessions, they obviously symbolize love and position to him.

One twenty-two-year-old woman broke an engagement and moved back into her mother's home when her mother remarried a man with two teenage girls. Did she want to monitor her mother's affection and make sure she got her fair share? Most likely.

On the other hand, we have seen stepsiblings grow into loving and loyal friends. The experience for them is enriching and fun. At least half of the stepchildren we interviewed who have been in a merged family for more than three years describe the relationships with their stepsiblings as positive. For them it's a good addition, an "extra" for which they are grateful.

But, again, we have seen the nurturers marry the discounters and have watched the children with backgrounds of sparse love and shaky self-esteem systematically bringing down a stepsibling. Parent and stepparent often stand by, helplessly watching the process. If the parent steps in, taking sides unfairly, paying the stepchildren back in spades, the conflict is likely to be escalated. However, if the parent separates the children and finds out as objectively as possible the immediate cause of a fight, it may reduce the likelihood of escalation.

All too often, we have seen parents refrain from defending their own child, fearful of what the stepsiblings may do to the child when the parent is not there.

Sometimes parent and stepparent enter into the children's competition, each hoping to prove his children better than the other's. Rather than accepting and encouraging the differences in the children, the parent and stepparent can thereby create competition and unnecessary rivalry.

The maturity of the husband and wife, the strength of their relationship, makes or breaks the situation. No one can always be totally even and totally fair, but parents and stepparents can set up structures and see that the family functions as best it can within them. Neutral rules fairly enforced, truthful praise given each child, whenever possible, the lack of derogatory comparisons—all these help to defuse the step rivalry.

Half-siblings can also constitute an enormous threat to a stepchild. Just as the child is adjusting to the family, along comes this other character. Unlike the stepchild, this one belongs to both parents. His position has got to be stronger than that of the child of the old marriage, and the stepchild senses this. Also, the coming of the child puts a further stamp of permanence on this alien marriage.

"It wasn't really the marriage itself," says eighteen-year-old Guy, both of whose parents remarried people who had never been married before and proceeded to have one and two children respectively. "It was that they had children. That's where it breaks down. I felt alienated from those kids. My sister and brother, all of us, were jealous of them.

"I don't like little kids anyway. I guess I'm sort of rude. I say, 'Would you pop him in the oven?' and stuff like that. I don't know whether I would lift a finger to help either of my stepmother's kids if they were in trouble.

"My brother, who's in college, fantasizes about getting rid of them totally. His feeling is more monetary. How many ways can you split this up, five kids rather than three?"

One tool parents can use to disperse sibling rivalry is reinforcement of good behavior. When siblings, stepsiblings, half-siblings treat each other well, parents and stepparents could acknowledge the good behavior and reward it, with mention made and attention paid to the act.

REINFORCING GOOD BEHAVIOR

Giving the child the attention he or she needs, and spoiling the child are confusing issues to many parents. The issue also becomes more acute in the stepfamily. For all the reasons we already know: there's usually more bad behavior, more testing, more acting out, more sullenness, etc., in the stepchild. Therefore the reinforcement of good behavior is especially important in step.

Reinforcement, of course, works both ways. Parents may

unwittingly reinforce upsetting behavior by nagging, yelling, or being angry. To the child, angry attention paid an act is better than no attention at all.

According to Dr. Philip Nelson, "Some people don't know how to give rewards. Parents, and this is a common thing, don't understand—don't look at—what they are doing in terms of their interaction with children. Take a couple of kids and a busy mother. If the two kids start fighting, mother runs in and interacts with them, thereby reinforcing what they are doing. By the same token, if the two are really enjoying each other, mother's reaction is, Thank God, they're being good, I'm going to get my ironing done, and she leaves the room. What happens is that the children get reinforced for fighting—mother's attention is contingent upon hassling and fighting. When they are playing cooperatively, they get ignored. Punishing two kids for fighting in no way teaches them how to be cooperative. Watching for cooperative behavior and reinforcing it, does.

"It often happens with a stepparent who comes in and doesn't care much for the child. The stepparent tends to ignore the child except when the child is being mean or destructive or unpleasant. Then the stepparent spanks or scolds or punishes. In such a case the whole interaction with the stepparent is a negative thing. Often the child wants the new parent very much, but the only way the child can get an interaction from the new parent is by doing something wrong.

"Something is happening that is very clear," says Dr. Nelson. "Kids as well as adults want to be loved, really want to be loved. They are set up with the idea that the parent should love a child. A child believes, 'My parent or stepparent must love me.' What happens when a child believes that a parent must love him, and he finds his parents being very abusive and angry and always criticizing, is that he has a dissonance. The child resolves the dissonance by linking the two together. A parent loving me means a parent doing this, being nasty, and it carries right on into adulthood. It creates a need for that kind of attention —negative."

By being aware of the phenomenon, a parent or stepparent can alter behavior. It takes a little thinking, a little control, and a little planning; but it can work. By deciding what they do want from these children, a parent and stepparent can go about getting it.

Another way to alter behavior is to model the kind of behavior desired. The parent and stepparent model for the children what it is to be a man or a woman, what it is to be in love, what it is to raise a family. They demonstrate various ways of being and behaving. The children will pick up a system of ethics, a philosophy of living, a style of acting and reacting. These are the patterns that go on through life. Being the model for these patterns is parenting in its truest sense.

SEX AND STEP

Upon the remarriage of a parent, the sexuality in the new marriage is more evident to the stepchild. Had the couple been married before the child was born, the groans and moans from the marital bedroom probably would not be so loud by the time the child was old enough to take notice. We certainly don't advocate that the couple stop, but the parents need to be aware that the child may be upset by what's going on and take whatever precautions they can.

Susie recalls visiting the home of her father and his new wife over a school holiday and looking through the door of their bedroom, noticing that the sheets and blankets were in disarray. Everything was rumpled up. Pillows were in funny places, and blankets were on the floor. Often at night Susie would go to the kitchen after her father and stepmother were in bed and pass slowly by their closed door, listening. . . .

In the merged family, girls suddenly find themselves with brothers, and boys with sisters. They may find each other attractive and get involved in sex play, especially since the incest taboo is not wholly extended to step relations. Sometimes a stepbrother and stepsister marry each other.

One young man recalls the very special feelings he had for his younger stepsister:

"They were girls, and we were boys. We really worked at getting along with them, and we did.

"I fell in love with the very young one. She eventually fell in love with me. It was a dream that flickered across my heart for years.

"She's a beautiful girl, just beautiful. I waited a lot of years for her, staying away, just waiting. I waited until she was in college—then we loved and made love. It was a completely idealized thing."

Dr. Lenore Terr has frequently seen incest between stepsiblings. (She speaks of incest as being a much wider area of concern than just sexual intercourse.) Because the siblings are not blood relatives, they are more inclined to become sexually involved. If they do, they aren't happy about it; this sort of thing doesn't make anybody feel good. It's too convenient, too easy, and they *are* brother and sister. The guilt about sex or sex play can harm.

Dr. Terr believes that stepbrothers and stepsisters in their teens often need to be given a protected feeling at home. Perhaps an older woman could be invited into the home when the parents go out. A certain decorum, certain rules can be set up: no running around in underwear; after a certain hour everybody stays in his own room. Just as parents don't allow children to walk into their bedroom, children too can be given privacy. Or perhaps two girls can share a bedroom, each, in effect, acting as chaperone for the other.

Stepchildren can fall in love with their stepparents as well as with each other. Take the case of a teenage boy falling in love with his stepmother. He may fantasize sexually and romantically about her, only to experience massive guilt as well as overstimulation. First this woman is his father's wife (that may be part of the attraction); second, she's in a position of mother; third, loving her is disloyal to his own mother.

Outwardly he may react all sorts of ways. He may demonstrate great hostility toward his stepmother or he may withdraw, pretending disinterest. He may, on the other hand, become angry or rivalrous with his father. A younger child may simply follow his stepmother around and be exceedingly sensitive to any criticism. An older child may demand an inappropriate amount of physical affection. Dr. J. Louise Despert, a child psychiatrist and the author of *Children of Divorce,* recommends that the stepmother draw the lines gently but firmly. A kiss on the cheek instead of the mouth, a light hug instead of a tight hug. "Save it for your girl," a stepmother can say lightly to a teenage stepson in a cuddly mood.

One young boy wrote his stepmother a long, impassioned love letter from boarding school. He recalls years later his gratitude over the way she handled it. She and his father both wrote him a letter, saying how happy they were that he accepted his new stepmother, that she was equally delighted to have him for her new stepson. They wrote that they were in love, that his acceptance of their marriage meant a great deal to them. From that day on, he says, he put aside his romantic fantasies and settled into the role of son—relieved, but never knowing for certain whether or not his stepmother had actually understood the intent of his letter. A less mature handling of the situation might have embroiled the new family in difficulties.

For people to live together successfully in intimacy, there have to be sexual taboos. The incest taboo needs to be firmly extended to step situations. The effects of incest in step are severely damaging all the way around.

9

The Parent without Custody

TOM

It was two o'clock on a Sunday afternoon when the old familiar despair began to seep into him. Tom tried not to let it show. Mustn't let Ronnie experience any of it. He was such a happy child, such a wonderful boy.

At five o'clock he'd put him on the plane and send him back to his mother. Wave and smile the last good-bye—"See you next month"—and drive back to the empty apartment. He'd get through until it was time for his date; then maybe he could forget for a while.

He'd call Ronnie the next day or so. The loneliness was always worst just before and after he left. Tom always kept in touch—postcards, short (very short) letters, telephone calls. The idea was to let Ronnie know that Tom was still his dad, that he was still behind him one hundred percent.

Sometimes his phone bill would run $80 a month. The air fare was another $80 for the monthly weekend visit. But it was worth every penny. Besides, he didn't waste money buying Ronnie gifts and junk. At first, when he was really strapped with the alimony, he'd always tried to give Ronnie a present whenever he saw him. Grace had said, "You don't have to do that. You don't want him to look at your visits as a time to get something instead of someone." She'd been right. It was a mistake to set yourself up as a supplier of things rather than warmth and friendship and parenting.

The telephone calls, translated into things, would amount to quite a bit. Ronnie would be glutted with gifts but unhappy and unsatisfied. The calls allowed a continuity of communication.

Well, maybe it was more than continuity; sometimes he'd ache so much for the boy, miss him so much, that he'd call just to hear his voice. On some of those calls Ronnie would be bubbling over and eager to talk. Other times he'd be busy with a friend, or eating dinner, or watching television, and wouldn't want to stay on the phone. He tried to understand and not feel slighted. Ronnie had his own life.

The divorce, that shattering of his family, was the hardest thing that had ever happened to Tom. He'd wake up in the middle of the night thinking about it—it had been five years now, but still the pain kept returning.

Just because his wife had wanted something different. He'd been a gentleman about it. He loved Ronnie so much; he'd done his best to make it work. He wondered if Grace would ever realize what she'd done to him and to Ronnie. She'd gotten what she'd wanted, an exciting and glamorous life. But at what a cost! Both he and Ronnie had a hole in the middle of their lives.

Maybe she did too. She hinted at trouble with the stepchildren, trouble between her husband and Ronnie. She'd cried once, talking about Christmas. She said second families were never the same, and Christmas was the worst of all. She'd offered him Ronnie for Christmas: "It doesn't matter any more."

But how could he give Ronnie a decent Christmas? Two people alone? Dinner in a restaurant? True, they'd had one wonderful Christmas back when he was dating Eleanor. An old-fashioned Christmas tree, turkey, presents, her two children, Ronnie, eggnog, the two of them, the works. Then the snow had come and Ronnie couldn't get back in time for school. Eleanor had taken care of Ronnie for a week while he worked. She'd been a good sport about it. No splitting there—everyone had come away richer for that relationship. Probably Grace didn't have the openness of spirit Eleanor had. But then Eleanor didn't have Grace's style.

"How about a game of chess, Ronnie? Think you can beat your old man?"

"Sure, Dad. This time you're my pigeon." Ronnie ran to get the set.

"You set it up. We've got time for a minor tournament before we leave for the airport."

On the way to the airport they talked about things they'd done that weekend. Washing and waxing the car together. Playing squash. Sanding and oiling the old chest they'd bought together last month. Visiting the Kramers and playing Monopoly. Cooking a superb breakfast of sausages and eggs. Dinner at a supper theater—a great version of *Sherlock Holmes.* Reading together some Holmes stories, each of them outdoing the other in his theatrical reading style. Starting a complicated airplane model, a helicopter they'd have to finish next month. And next month they'd paint the den, Ronnie's room whenever he was with his father. . . .

"So long, wonderful boy! See you soon!"

"So long, Dad! Don't lose any of the helicopter parts. Tell Miss Renshaw goodbye. And don't forget to buy the blue paint! See you!"

Clunk . . . clunk, clunk, clunk. He felt heavy inside.

Tom walked to his new car. What good was all the success without someone to share it with? Maybe if he married again, he could get Ronnie for a year. Maybe Grace would agree to let them have him for high school. He was dreaming! Grace would never give him up.

He had to admit she was a good mother, and she never talked against him, lessened him in Ronnie's eyes. Nor did she try to get Ronnie to look at his stepfather as his father. Neither of them did that. Thank God.

Basically, it was good that Grace had married John. He'd never tried to take his place as father. He let Ronnie know he respected his dad. Tom, in turn, did his part. Once, when they were driving in the car, Ronnie had said, "I have the best dad, and the best mom, and the best stepdad in the whole world." They'd made a little game of it after that, chanting: "The best dad, the best mom, the best stepdad."

Grace would complain about John's treatment of Ronnie, but he'd never seen any cause for complaint, and Ronnie seemed to have only good things to say about his stepfather.

At first Tom had been concerned that Grace's husband would attempt to take his son from him. He'd put it in the separation agreement that there would be no adoption, that Ronnie would always carry his name. When Grace had first gotten married, Ronnie started calling Tom by his first name. He'd say, "Call me Dad. I'm the only person in the world you can honestly call Dad, so call me that." But there hadn't been a problem. John hadn't tried to be Dad.

John provided a good home for Grace and Ronnie. That was something. Tom had gotten out from under the alimony, but he'd never forget the grubby struggle of those first two and a half years. Worrying about Ronnie, never knowing how or when it would end, just so Grace could find that "something else" she wanted. Maybe if, when they were married, Tom hadn't worked so hard, had been less of an m.c.p., considered . . . Maybe if she had found the work she wanted. . . .

"Stop it, Tom," he told himself. The beauty of life was that you kept going forward, every day a new dimension. Sure, you limped a little, but . . . He thought he'd try that new restaurant tonight with Elizabeth. Now there was an elegant woman, steel fist in white glove, courage *and* wit, attractive. . . .

He wondered if Ronnie would make the connection at the other end without a hitch. Why should there be a hitch? There had been five years of travel. Travel. That's what he'd do. He'd take Ronnie to California this summer. They'd camp at Yosemite, go down to San Diego. . . .

DICK

"Look," Dick told her, "as long as these children are on my payroll, they're going to wear their hair the way I say."

"Will you listen to me?" shouted his ex-wife. "Their long hair is their security with the other kids! Jeffrey [age ten] cried every morning for a week, refusing to go to school the last time you made him get a haircut. He was humiliated."

"They look like bums. Filthy hippies. Every time I pick them up you're off somewhere, and the kids are dirty—dirty clothes, dirty fingernails, and dirty hair. I told them I won't take them out for dinner next week if they look like that."

"Off somewhere! I'll tell you why I'm off somewhere. I'm off somewhere because I have to be somewhere and you're an hour or two late. And they've nothing to do but sit there hungry and fighting while they wait for you."

"Does it ever occur to you that I have to work, and that certain responsibilities might delay me? What's to stop you from giving them a snack or organizing something for them to do while they wait? And as long as you're on my payroll you better start trying to manage a . . ."

"Payroll. You and your payroll. Why don't you think in terms of YOUR responsibilities instead of salaries or something? And what about the clothes for camp? The bill came to $195 for the three of them, and . . ."

"God damn it! Why don't you read your contract? You get the child support, and you pay for the clothes. Stop trying to nickel and dime me to death."

He slammed the door and bolted for the car. Most disorganized woman in the world. Had no sense of what a contract was, an agreement between two people that was to be lived by. Maybe he'd better get his lawyer to show her.

Those were the children she'd wanted. Every one of them had been her idea. And now she wanted him to take responsibility without even having custody.

God, it made him mad to see those kids out of control. Dirty. No manners. Barely even saying thank you for all the things he did with them and all the gifts he gave them.

But what could you expect with a mixed-up mother like that? Christ, she was on his payroll and he couldn't even fire her.

She was better, though, since she'd gotten remarried. Although it infuriated him the way that fool husband of hers took an unhealthy amount of interest in his boys. Always meddling. Interfering. Upsetting things.

HARRY

Harry's children come to visit under considerable strain. His Alex is very antagonistic, picking up all the nuances of antagonisms from his mother. He is bitter, hateful, and unpleasant. Alex is twelve now. Harry's younger girls, Jenny and Sandy, aged nine and seven, are less of a problem.

Alex's hostility is a direct reflection of his mother's feelings, and it's tied in with financial insecurity and her expression of these things to the children. They have picked up great antagonism in feeling that Harry has not provided enough for them.

Alex has been involved to such an emotional degree that he has telephoned Harry and his new wife with the most hysterical anger and accusations for not providing this or that, for not providing for him or his sisters or his mother. Once he even called to say that his mother wasn't eating dinner that night because Harry hadn't given enough money. Harry feels she funnels her accusations through the boy, causing him to want to protect her the only way he can, by going after his father.

It upsets Harry that his former wife has made no attempt to protect the children from her feelings or from any encounter between the two of them. Harry continues to protest, to no avail, that their disagreements should be in private and are not a matter for the children. She responds that the children have to learn about real life.

Each week Harry hopes to make it better. Each week he's more and more discouraged. He knows that Alex has been seriously hurt. Whether he will heal he's not sure. Harry fears his relationship with his son will be destroyed if he doesn't do something. Yet what should he do?

There are moments when Harry feels horrifying despair. You can't stop kids from absorbing their environment. So he is prepared, not really emotionally prepared, but at least intellectually geared to realizing that he may lose his children. He can't take them away from their mother, though he feels he should. But, on legal grounds, these things are difficult to prove. Still he feels what is going on is horrendously damaging to the children.

JANE

Jane used to worry continually about her ten-year-old son, Jimmy. He stuttered, had difficulty in school, and was always hanging his head. He had seemed to be stumbling through his life.

Holding down her job, covering the rent, getting Jimmy to the therapist, the tutor, forever making arrangements for Jimmy, worrying about finding time to enjoy her daughter, Jill (who didn't seem to have any problems), keeping up some social life—Jane had been beside herself.

On weekends when she finally had some time, they would go to her former husband's house in the country. Jane would take the children to Grand Central Station on Friday nights, feeling shredded to pieces. Then she'd wait for them there on Sunday nights, worrying, hoping everything was all right.

It was the therapist who first got her to consider the possibility that she might reverse the situation. Fred and Maude could have the children during the week and she could have them on weekends. "No!" she had cried. That would mean giving up custody. She could never do that. It wouldn't be right.

Still, she never knew what was going to happen next with Jimmy. There had been another letter from the landlord saying that somebody was throwing eggs out the window of her apartment. Before that it had been firecrackers. Jimmy had had reading problems and it was likely that he would have to stay back again the following year or go to a special private school.

Life had never been easy after the divorce. She had received decent child support, but it hadn't seemed to be enough. The problems with Jimmy had really begun with the divorce. Poor Jimmy. At five, he'd lost a father and gained a baby sister. All at once. He'd never really recovered.

Fred had been upset after every visit of the children. Several times he had asked her to let them live with him.

One summer after the children had been to Arizona on a vacation with their father and stepmother, Fred had called Jane and asked if Jill and Jimmy could stay with them for the rest of the summer. The children hadn't wanted to come back to the city, so Jane had agreed.

At the end of that summer, Jane had brought Jimmy back to the city for a doctor's appointment. He'd been having asthma attacks. As they drove around for forty-five minutes looking for a parking place, Jimmy had started in on how he hated the city —the air, the traffic, the weird people.

Something had clicked. School would be starting soon. Jimmy couldn't go back to the public school. She had called Fred. "Do you still want the kids to live with you?"

About this time she had gotten over her anger with Fred and Maude. Maude was a nice person, had a good relationship with both kids, and was the kind of woman who was naturally good with children.

It was August. All the psychologists had seemed to be out of town. They had scrambled around trying to find a child psychologist to advise them on how to tell the children. The man they had talked with suggested that they tell the children about it as though the decision were final. Of course, if it didn't work out, they could always change the arrangements; but the children should not be made to feel that the choice was up to them.

Jane had told them. It was okay with Jill. Jimmy was surprised. Jane had started to cry. Jimmy said, "Oh, that's sad." He had been anxious about when and under what circumstances they would see each other, but he said that he liked Maude and would try it.

For the first three years, Jane saw the children basically every weekend. At first she brought the children into the city to spend the weekends with her in the apartment. Now it was she who did all the fun things—cooked special meals, took them to movies, whatever. She was doing what Fred had done. And most of the time it was great being freed from the daily hassles of single motherhood in the city.

As the kids grew older, they didn't want to leave home every weekend. Jane began to visit them in the country. Things were calm and peaceful in the suburb. Jane used to wonder why she couldn't have such a life, yet she didn't really want it. She liked her life in the city. They'd all have dinner together, and she'd talk with Maude about what had gone on during the week. She and Maude would also talk a couple of times each week on the phone.

Maude was nice, easy to be around, and very fair. She didn't try to push Jane out of her place as mother, and Jane considered the children lucky to have her. Maude never would have been a friend of hers by choice—she wasn't that interesting—but she was good with the children. It was what she liked to do.

Things went along reasonably well until Jimmy got suspended from school. Maude and Fred started suggesting that Jane see the children less. They were upset after her visits. Both Maude and Fred implied that Jane didn't have enough things going on in her life and that the children felt sorry for her. He accused her of only entertaining the children—never taking responsibility. He said all the things she remembered having said to him.

Finally, they all calmed down. They went together to see Jimmy's psychologist. Maude and Fred said they felt they were living in a fishbowl. Jane tried to understand how they must feel. She tried listening to them rather than repeating her own position various ways, and she agreed to see the children every other weekend in the city instead of every weekend in the country. They would all be flexible. If either Maude or the children or Jane had conflicting plans, they'd change things around. Maude and Fred agreed that Jimmy might have been playing Maude/Fred and Jane against each other.

Next weekend Jane will drive up to the country and visit her ex-mother-in-law. She'll see Jimmy for a while, perhaps talk to Maude. She and Maude now respect each other's rights. If they get upset on the telephone, they say they'll call back. Neither tries to get hooked into the position of being right. The children are doing well.

Jane has gotten over those waves of hate she used to feel when she put the children on the train to go back to the country. Sometimes she wishes she had more control over the children's lives, but she speaks up when she feels something is important. Jane tries not to be trapped by the guilt-inducing stereotype as to what divorced mothers should do. This is what she chose, and she feels responsible for the decision. She believes it's best for the children as well as herself.

Jane is looking forward to taking the children on a trip across the country next summer. They have such wonderful times when the three of them are alone together. . . .

FRUSTRATION AND LONELINESS

Before writing this book, we felt that the parent without custody was the person in the step constellation who had the easiest time of it, while the rest were left to cope. After all, some parents just vanish; others come around spasmodically at best. Oddly enough, the more absent they are, the more their children tend to forgive and idealize them. Nevertheless, the majority of parents without custody have assumed an extremely difficult and often painful role. Feelings of loss, powerlessness, frustration, guilt, and loneliness abound. Often this parent finds himself making accommodation after accommodation after accommodation. It may well be the toughest of all the step positions.

Loss of custody, say many parents, is the beginning of the loss of control—especially in the case of the hostile ex-wife or -husband. A parent may be unhappy with the way the children are being raised and be powerless to do much about it. It may be difficult even to see the children, much less have an easy, natural relationship.

When the ex remarries, the parent without custody is presented with the hard fact of a new person in his old place. This other person is his day-to-day replacement in the home with his children. And he didn't even choose the person. At the same time, he still continues to pay out child support.

It hurts. A father hears his children calling another man Dad. Sometimes he hears them calling himself by his first name rather than Dad. One father wrote a letter to his former wife: "I have lost everything surrounding the relationship. At least let me keep my title and my name. Ask her to call me Dad, not Barry. Please."

I HAD TO WRITE THEM OFF

Many a father finds himself powerless to reverse hostilities engendered in the children by the mother (or a mother by the father). Unable or unwilling to take the antagonism, some parents simply give up the relationship.

One father told us, "I had to write them off. She'd done her work. Poisoned the children against me. I had to face what had taken place. They were something I had devoted a lot of my time and self to—a bad investment. I did the best I could. It didn't work. I have to look at it in those terms, or else it would tear me to pieces."

For others the relationship is firm and cannot be destroyed. "She tried to turn the boy against me," one father said. "She couldn't. I had roots with the boy. He was my son, and there was no taking that away."

It cannot be denied that two homes may amount to less than one; that where custody is split, a child has lost the necessary continuity of home and parent. Visits from the parent without custody do disrupt the basic relationship in the child's home; they sensitize conflicts and undermine the sense of belonging.

In the controversial book *Beyond the Best Interests of the Child* Anna Freud, along with co-authors Joseph Goldstein and Albert J. Selnit, states that whether a parent without custody be legally allowed to visit his children should be solely at the discretion of the parent with custody. They go so far as to say that the absent parent—if the parent with custody so desires—should be legally prevented from seeing his children. They argue that this would enable the natural parent and spouse to bring up the child without conflict from this now absent parent. They maintain that court-ordained visitations are an official invitation to disrupt the unbroken continuity of affection and relationship that a child must have with at least one parent in the home. The authors reason, "Loyalty conflicts are common and normal under such conditions and may have devastating consequences by destroying the child's positive relationships to both parents."

KEEPING UP THE RELATIONSHIP

Nevertheless, most experts would not suggest that a loving parent give up contact with his or her children. Keeping up the continuity of the relationship and contact with the child is one of the major concerns of a parent separated from his children. We suggest that visits or communications of the parent without custody be regular, and something the child can count on. Tom's story illustrates this. Too frequently, we see parents who go for long periods of time without contacting a child, or they will only get in touch with the child on a helter-skelter basis.

THE BALANCE OF DISCIPLINE

The parent without basic custody often is confused about the area of discipline. We have seen parents who underdiscipline and turn away from outrageous behavior. Fearing the further loss of an already diminished relationship, they may not correct the obvious. Then there are parents who overdiscipline, getting involved in lengthy harangues over matters which really no longer are in their control.

Connecticut psychiatrist Dr. Leon Tec stated his views regarding the disciplinary role of a parent who sees a child periodically:

"The parent who visits doesn't discipline, except for the things that happen in front of him. If he sees a child take a stone and throw it at a dog, he will say, 'Please don't throw stones. I think that's cruel. I don't like it.' But that's the limit: it is defined by what happens at the time, not before or after the visit.

"As far as hair length and manner of dress, the same thing applies. The parent who does not live with a child cannot express a demand. He can express a preference. He can say, 'I like it when your hair is short.' 'I like clean clothes.' 'I like it when you wear slacks and not blue jeans.' Always 'I's.' And always 'my preference.' "

ON NOT BECOMING AN ENTERTAINMENT CENTER

Life becomes less frustrating for the parent who can provide a place for extended visits with the children. Now they are there in that parent's home. The parent is the man or woman of that house, not the absentee father or mother.

Now discipline becomes easier. The "rules of the house" concept can again be invoked: In this house we wear clean clothes at dinner, hold the obscenities to a minimum, and so on. The house rules of each home may be different. That's okay. But this is the way it is here.

The method works, but partial custody can be difficult all the same. Weekly visitation can be even more difficult. There the parent usually is attempting in short spurts to maintain or build a parental relationship out of the context of the child's ongoing household. Such a parent can fall into a familiar scenario.

Let's see. It's twelve o'clock. They've been to the zoo (somehow it's always the zoo), the park, and a restaurant for lunch. Now they have two hours to go. The ice-cream cones they are about to buy can't possibly fill up the two hours. Next Sunday won't be much different. Parent and child often get bored, tired, and restless.

A basic mistake has been made. A parent is not an entertainer. Relationships are not enhanced by a series of ball games, movies, and museums. The parental function is being sidestepped. What is important is that the parent be there for the child. The time spent together should not comprise hectic efforts to entertain him.

We recommend the kind of activities that Tom enjoyed with his son Ronnie. They did normal household chores together—raking leaves, washing the car, mowing the lawn, cooking. They also chose activities in which there is room for an interchange—working at the workbench, building a model, playing checkers, making things—and enjoyed the occasional special outing (the "great version" of *Sherlock Holmes*). Also there was time to talk and share their feelings and thoughts with each other.

Too much of what the child wants leaves the parent irritable. Too much of what only the parent wants will leave the child eager for the visit to be over. There should be a mix of activities they both enjoy. If it is not a geographic impossibility, the father or mother should get involved in basic kinds of activities, such as going to school nights. The parent will feel more a part of things.

With some children it's best to keep visits short and frequent, if at all possible. It may be a good idea to take the children one at a time every so often and get to know them individually instead of as a unit. On occasion it's good to have the child bring along a friend, or to find friends for the child nearby.

Dr. Philip Nelson of Denver puts it this way: The parent needs to relate as a parent and not as someone who shows the children a good time all the time. Parents without custody tend to overcompensate. They do it not only through overentertainment but through overindulgence and excessive gift giving as well. The parent without custody may be attempting to buy the child's love or loyalty or to make up for his absence.

The parents themselves set this up—seeing who can do the most for the child—and the child uses it. The child may play the two parents against each other, or the parents may use the child against each other. There's one certain result: everybody loses.

With divorced parents who support each other, who manage their difficulties with each other without running them through the child, the situation is very different indeed. Under these circumstances, there's a chance at least of everybody gaining something.

10

The Parent with Custody

NANCY COULD WRITE all the words in red, she thought: split, tear, cut, separate, divide, decide, choose. Write them on the blade of a silver knife and give them to her husband.

She needed to be one whole, not two halves split between husband and children, giving separately—almost furtively—to each. Why did she always feel she had to separate them? Keep the kids away from her husband, so he wouldn't become annoyed, so they wouldn't get rejected. Why did she always have to feel guilty—guilty if she spent time alone with her children being a good mother, guilty if she spent time alone with her husband feeding her marriage?

She was always dividing it up—time for the children, then her husband, then the children again, then Bruce again. She felt Bruce acted as if it were a normal family only when his two girls, Margie and Tory, were with them.

In the normal family one of the ways you loved your husband was through loving your children. They were his children too, and loving them was part of your love for your husband. But Bruce looked at her love for her children as a betrayal of their own stormy love. No doubt about it, her children were the monkey wrench in her marriage. And her marriage got in the way of her relationship with Bobby and Kim.

The surprise of it all. She'd thought marrying Bruce would solve her mothering problems, that he'd give her steadiness and strength and comfort. Instead, Bruce and the kids seemed to be tearing her apart.

It's either/or, she thought. Either Bruce, or Bobby and Kim. When Bobby and Kim would go to camp for two months, and she and Bruce were alone, everything was fine. Their fights would fade, along with the turbulence inside herself.

It was the same when Bruce went on a business trip. She and Bobby and Kim would be a family again. Happy, relaxed, laughing, spontaneous. They'd have wonderful times together, picnicking in the backyard, making fudge in the kitchen, never worrying about pleasing or displeasing Bruce. And somehow when she wasn't trying to shove the kids into the background to pacify Bruce, they didn't make so many demands. But she'd know when Bruce was on his way home. Bobby would hear his car coming up the driveway and would run into the house making the sounds of a submarine in trouble.

Put them all together—say, at the dinner table—and things could feel downright precarious. There she'd be in the middle, engineering, trying to see that Bruce wouldn't be angered and Bobby wouldn't be rejected. She didn't have to worry so much about Kim; Kim seemed to know how to handle Bruce.

Sometimes she'd sit at the table wondering. Are these two my children, and this my husband, all sitting here stiff as boards, trying to have a decent conversation for my benefit? Is this really my family? And she'd try to steer the conversation around to make it more natural.

Bruce would put down Bobby—by ignoring him, by not responding to something he'd said, or by jerking his shoulders in annoyance whenever Bobby said anything. The more Bruce ignored him, the harder Bobby would try. She'd have to pay particular attention to Bobby to make up for Bruce. Then Bruce would say that Bobby was a weird kid, always dominating their dinners and getting her attention for his antics.

There was a competition between them. Bobby and Bruce would each try to show in some small or big way—you name it—that he was the best. Once she'd told Bobby that there was no way he could beat out that grown man; why didn't he wait until he was grown? Bobby had said Bruce would be too old by then.

She'd laughed. And she thought of what the psychiatrist had told her, "Nine out of ten stepfathers don't have the maturity not to be jealous of their stepsons."

"A grown man like Bruce?" she'd asked.

"Sure," he'd answered with a smile.

There was the competition between all of them—Bobby, Kim, and Bruce—for her time and attention. It was simply incredible that this big, powerful man should be jealous of two little kids. Why did he invest them with so much power? Her tempestuous Othello. She could have an affair with the garbage man, and it wouldn't stir him up as much as it did when she paid particular attention to her children or spoke with her first husband, Carl.

Either/or? Neither/nor? She simply could not go on separating herself, walking the taut rope of her loyalties, keeping the whole act balanced. But how could she be happy if she gave up Bruce? She'd never forgive the children. How could she live if she gave up custody of her own children? She'd never forgive Bruce.

So here she stood. Crying like some crazy lady in her kitchen. Fantasizing about writing words in red nail polish on one of her silver knives. . . .

THE CONFLICT OF LOYALTIES

Nancy's feelings are shared by many parents, male and female, with custody in the stepfamily. Many of them have said that they feel pulled in opposite directions in their efforts to fulfill the needs of both their children and their spouse. Feeling a sense of conflicting loyalties, they often find themselves in the middle, engineering the reactions of each to the other. The result is a building of fences rather than bridges between the family members.

A mother, for example, will put herself in the middle between husband and children. She attempts to maneuver the child to act in a certain way. "Go kiss Martin goodnight." To her husband she says, "Johnny would like it if you'd . . ."

She wants the marriage to work. She wants the children to be happy. She revs up her efforts to forge the relationships and often unwittingly enforces further separation.

We have been told, especially by stepfathers, that often when they're left alone with the child things go better. For one, the element of the inevitable competition is removed. For another, the manipulating has stopped. And then people left alone have to forge some kind of interaction.

Many mothers and some fathers feel that they cannot trust their mate to deal nurturingly with their child. They can cite incident after incident to back up their feelings. Often, however, the parent feels the stepparent is being indifferent or unfair toward a child when the child isn't even feeling it. The child, we've frequently found, is unperturbed by, say, the stepfather's behavior that so upsets the mother. "That's just the way he is," the child will say with a shrug.

Differing perceptions of the same scene were illustrated to us one day over lunch with a friend. She was worried for her children, feeling that they weren't getting what they needed from their stepfather. "I know that I am the sole emotional support of my children," she said. "Of course, he does sports and things with them, but he never puts them on his knee and lets them know he cares about them."

The next week (we had license to snoop; we were writing this book), we interviewed one of her children. The boy thought his stepfather was just great—loved his athletic involvement, and so on.

"Do you ever think he doesn't like you?" we asked.

"I *know* he likes me."

"How do you know?"

"Because every night when he says goodnight to me, he says, 'I love you, man.' "

Men and women have different styles of nurturing. Of course, one has sympathy with the lone parent's position. Her child is her most vulnerable place. She worries about his development, his self-confidence, his feelings.

Rejection of one's child feels like rejection of oneself. We are in actuality calling out to our spouse and lover to love all of us—including the children. The spouse may translate that to

"She loves these children more than me." Misinterpreted emotions abound, of course, in intact families and in human relationships generally. But in step that same dynamic of misrelating is enlarged by the step relationship. What may be tolerable in an intact family becomes distended out of proportion in step.

The mother-child tie is extremely strong, almost inevitably. If that relationship is violated, insulted, or put down, the biological parent is going to get back at the stepparent, whether consciously or not. A wounded mother protecting her children can be vicious indeed.

Sometimes a mother feels she doesn't have the strength to protect her children alone. If her husband can't help her, the marriage may not last. This was the case with a woman we interviewed who told us about a recurring dream.

Her house was on fire. It was night, and her child was sleeping on a different floor. Her husband, the stepfather, ran outside, calling her to come with him. The child was screaming, pinned under a heavy beam on the floor below. In the dream she ran to the child, wasn't strong enough to lift the beam, called out frantically to her husband. She needed his strength to lift the beam, to save the child. Her husband only yelled at her to get out of there. She had the dream repeatedly. She felt she could not trust her husband to be there for her and her child. The marriage broke up after a year.

THE STEPPARENT WHO DISCOUNTS THE CHILD

The struggle can be enormous—often seemingly without results. One mother tells of her early efforts, her early requests that seemed to fall on deaf ears . . . until she found herself shouting her needs:

"My ten-year-old boy dies every day for a nod of approval from his stepfather. That first year of our marriage Sammy got barely anything you could call emotionally supportive from Hal. Ten-speed bikes and trips—there were enough of those. But they don't count as replacements for love not given.

"Sammy was basically treated like some sort of human garbage that Hal had to deal with in the house—'oh, uggh' was the meaning of all his moves and messages toward my son. We'd never dealt with people like that in our family. I just couldn't believe what was happening here in our beautiful new house with the love of my life.

"All he ever communicated to the boy was *don't*—all in the negative pluperfect tense of nervous dislike. If Sammy wasn't doing something Hal disliked, Hal would ignore him until Sammy would whine or do something bad, so Hal could dislike him. I ran around in circles trying to put patches on the relationship, while Hal swung my son around like a cat with a mouse.

"It's not surprising that Sammy got wiggly and antsy. He'd try to get Hal's attention, show him things he'd done in school that day. He could count on what he'd get—damned little. 'That's nice, now go away.' Or 'Later, later, can't you see I'm busy?'

"My loving man had turned into a mind-messing monster to all else I had in this world, my son. When it came down to it, I had some good work in magazines and TV commercials, but in reality only Sammy had I produced. He was the bottom line of my midlife report—literally the pride of my life.

"One night Hal came home just before Sammy had to go to bed. Since he had only a few moments to spend with the boy, he could relax and spend a few warm minutes with him. Hal is capable of charming the Guccis off an Italian princess if he sets himself to it. This night, all he had to do was acknowledge one thing Sammy had done and say goodnight.

"Sammy and I gleefully gave Hal the news: Sammy had scored two goals in soccer that had made him the high goal scorer of his grammar school.

"Hal's response? 'That Phil Braden is a lousy soccer coach.' That was it; that was all. Dumbstruck again, I returned with 'Oh, you, you don't know anything about coaching.'

"Later that night, Hal kissed me and hugged me and told me once again how much he loved me. He wanted to make love. There was no way. How could he turn me on when he had so successfully just turned off my son? I pushed him away, but he pursued me, thinking I was just playing difficult. 'No, no, no,' I said and began to whimper. 'Don't you see that all that child needs is love and attention, just like you, like any human being? And don't you see that he's too little not to be permanently hurt by your putdowns?'

"At that point, Hal could have offered to try with Sammy, and have taken me in his arms again. But no. 'Always that damned kid of yours,' he says, and attempts to brush the whole thing away by pulling me closer. 'No!' This time I shouted and shoved him away.

"It could happen any night. One night we had a free-for-all over how bad his children were and how awful Sammy was. We each accused the other's and defended our own. We were like a couple of five-year-olds arguing about whose daddy was stronger. Neither of us could believe it, but we got deeper and deeper into it.

"The next day was a Sunday. Sammy had taken in some gerbils for a friend who had gone away for the weekend. He announced the fact to Hal. 'Oh, Hal, go and look at them,' I said. 'They're so cute.'

"Hal went—then he let loose. 'We're not going to have any pets in this house. How dare you bring anything here without asking me first!' And so forth.

"Sammy began to cry, trying to explain, but the barrage was too much for him. They were both in Sammy's room, but I could hear what was going on.

"When I got there, Sammy was sitting rigid and scared silent. I pounced. 'The gerbils are just here for the weekend. I said he could take care of them. Of course I said he could. You're not the only one who can say what goes on around here.' The venom of the past began to surge through my veins. I carried it further. 'You jerk. What do you think you're doing raising your ill-founded voice at my son? Why don't you go out and fight with the big boys and lay off little kids? I think you're a monster as a parent. I have no respect for your judgment.'

"All the words and insults that had been stored up spewed forth right there in front of the gerbils and in front of Sammy. I grabbed Sammy and pulled him into another room, where I hugged him. We both cried. Oh, my little boy, how I loved him!

So much pain, so much glory, so much love, so much pure being there in that one person. *No one* would crush that. I wouldn't let it happen."

SPEAKING OUT IN FRONT OF THE CHILD

What can a parent with custody do who feels that the emotional needs of a child or children aren't being met, but who still wants to keep the marriage going?

Dr. Richard Gardner advises a parent to speak right out in front of a child. To a stepparent ignoring a child, the parent could say, "It hurts me to see you ignoring Suzie when she says hello to you." To a stepparent disciplining a child excessively, the parent could say, "Stop! You're being too harsh. What she did didn't deserve all that."

At first this struck us as undermining the stepparent in front of the child. Shouldn't the issue be discussed privately with one's spouse? Dr. Gardner's response: "Sure, you could go behind the back of the child." Then he added, "But sometimes you should stand up for the child in front of him—let him know you're with him."

Dr. Gardner's point is well taken: if the stepparent is being unfair or unkind or uninterested, the child needs to know that his parent has not abandoned him. The child needs support. Parents can take care of themselves. Children often can't. Open discussion either alone or with the child often needs to take place repeatedly. The parent can run into the automatic-denial syndrome of the stepparent:

"It hurts me to see you ignoring Johnny."

"I wasn't ignoring him."

"He was trying to tell you something important to him, and you wouldn't even look up."

"Come on, I was trying to read."

"Next time, please, for me, give him a few minutes of direct attention and then you can send him on his way."

Some parents, in an effort to protect the marriage, refuse to see what is happening—or they see it but somehow do little about it. Or, seeing it, they figure the child will survive, cope, surmount. Children are so resilient, you know. . . . Many such parents remember the failure of another marriage or relationship and want, at all costs, to keep this one intact.

OVERCOMPENSATING

Other parents attempt to make up for the lack of nurturing by overcompensating. Such a parent, seeing the stepparent indifferent toward a child, will attempt through his or her own attentions to make up for the lack. It goes like this: A mother (or father) feels a stepfather (or stepmother) is ignoring her child. She lavishes attention on the child. The stepfather (rightly) feels excluded, and retaliates by further ignoring, punishing, putting down, or diminishing the child. The mother increases her attentions toward the child, which leads to increased rejections from his stepfather, which leads to increased attention by the mother, which leads to . . .

On and on it goes, and it needn't. The destructive cycle can be broken or at least made less disruptive if parent, stepparent, and possibly even the child recognize what is going on and talk about it, openly. The overcompensating parent who realizes what she or he is doing can stop. The retaliative stepparent can stop retaliating. At this point, the situation for parent, stepparent, and child can only improve.

It had been a beautiful concert. Children's voices in sweet unison. Bobby had sung the solo parts perfectly in his clear soprano. Nancy was driving home alone on a dazzling sun-struck day, holding her heart together in the loneliness of her maternal pride.

She *needed* somebody to share her joy in Bobby's achievement. Bruce would "yes-but" her. "Too bad he can't do that well in math." Or "I'd rather see him play football."

The music lingered in her ears. The beauty of the day hurt her. Something was at odds with so much loveliness. Why was she so alone? Alone with her worries. With her victories. There was only one other person in the world who could share these feelings—Carl, and he was off somewhere as usual. She'd almost go back to him just to break up this awful icy chunk of loneliness inside her. . . .

THE ALONENESS IN RAISING THE CHILD

The parent who isn't married to a child's other parent can experience a horrible aloneness in raising that child. Rarely does a stepparent dote. The parent has lost the doting partner.

Christmas and birthdays poignantly underscore the problem. Who but a parent can feel such pleasure at a child's expressions of pleasure or surprise? That other person simply doesn't feel the way you do about your child or your children. With whom can you rejoice when your child does something supremely well—or even medium well? It's strange, the sadness and aloneness that accompany not having somebody with whom to exult.

Or somebody to comfort you and share your child's problem. Or do something about it. Or make the decisions once in a while. Sometimes the parent isn't allowing the stepparent an equal participation. Sometimes the stepparent simply isn't interested, or reacts to problems with the aha-I-always-thought-there-was-something-wrong-with-the-kid syndrome.

A parent may try to cover up a child's deficiencies, or dismiss them, or deny their existence. A stepparent may be able to see them clearly. On the other hand, a parent may overworry a problem the stepparent can see is nothing serious. This difference in viewpoint can work to the stepfamily's advantage if husband and wife can each accept and understand the other's way of seeing. If they can't, the divergence in viewpoint can exacerbate feelings of aloneness and frustration for both parent and stepparent.

All too often, stepparents don't enter into the parent's concerns with the children. Genuine parental involvement—the spontaneous smiles, little hugs, expressions of interest that we take for granted in fathers and mothers—is missing. Well, maybe only a mother or father could love *that* child!

The parent often expects precisely that kind of involvement

from the stepparent and, as a result, asks for more than the stepparent can deliver.

Expecting too much, the parent becomes disappointed or angry, or encourages false behavior in the stepparent. We as parents often ask steppeople to express in some way what we feel they *should* be feeling. We ask for an artificial emotion and are annoyed when it comes out artificially or doesn't come out at all. We may simply have to learn to accept the involvement for just what it is, within the limits of the stepperson.

Some people are naturally nurturing and supportive; some easily understand and love kids; some are family oriented. For these, the merger comes more easily.

THE STEPPARENT WHO IS NOT GOOD WITH CHILDREN

Many simply aren't. Even before marriage, parents usually know whether or not a person will be good with the children. If the future spouse isn't likely to be good with the children, and the parent still wants the remarriage, he or she must recognize the package deal for what it is and go along with it, appreciating the good components.

Dr. Richard Gardner suggests that if you go ahead and marry someone who hasn't shown much interest in your children, you come right out and talk to them about it:

"Look, Joe is a nice guy, and I love him very much. I wish he were the kind of man who is really interested in children, but he isn't. Not all men are. I would like you to know that I wish he'd be more affectionate with you, but he isn't likely to be. You have Daddy and Uncle John, and you have me. . . ."

This way it's out in the open. The child understands where the deficiencies lie. He won't feel personally diminished by skimpy affection or attention from his stepparent, and he won't suffer the effects of unrealistic expectations.

THE COUPLE'S RELATIONSHIP IS PRIMARY

We have seen couples who have worked out their step problems, each of them sharing with the other concerns for the other's children, each offering what they can and feeling grateful for the help of the other.

There seems to be a common secret to their success. The couple has put themselves first. This means that, when there's a question of priorities, each spouse understands that the needs of the couple come first. The couple also understands their obligations toward the children and can meet them more successfully because of their commitment to each other. Husband and wife have put their ex-spouses behind them. They're a team, and they gear up together to cope. They're open with each other; they trust each other. Two people who have that sort of relationship can handle a *lot* of problems.

One successful stepfather and father with custody told us, "My first love, my first consideration is my wife. I have no doubt that I am her first consideration and love also. On that base we predicate our lives, and those of our children. Our marriage has withstood a lot of assaults from pressures that the kids have imposed. The children have profited from the strength of our relationship—that's been what they needed. The safety, the permanence are all based upon where my wife and I are."

Dr. Tec says: "Some people remarry to provide a father or a mother for their children. That's a mistake. You provide a husband or a wife for yourself. If that works, the rest will work out. If you marry for the children, you'll be disappointed in your marriage. And you won't be the only one; your children will be disappointed in their stepmother or stepfather as well."

All of this is not to suggest that couples with a strong relationship won't have tough times protecting their marriage from the consequences of bringing in children from a prior marriage. So it was for Rachel and Alan. Rachel is our southern friend whose story is told in Chapter 4. Rachel describes there the horrendously difficult times they had after Alan had obtained custody of his troubled eleven-year-old son, also called Alan. Rachel said, "If only I had known that this too shall pass."

THE FATHER WITH CUSTODY

Alan tells how it came to pass:

"The mistake we made was not getting custody of Alan sooner. He was two years old when his mother and I divorced. The court granted her custody until he was eighteen years old. The first couple of years after the divorce, I saw a great deal of Alan. We all lived in the same city. Then I moved east, my ex-wife moved west, and things fell apart. Rachel and I were married, and we would see Alan for three, six, or eight weeks in the summer. It wasn't enough.

"Alan's mother is an older, attractive woman—and an alcoholic. Currently she's hospitalized for alcoholism. Alan's fantasy for a long time was that she would get better and he would be able to live with her half of the time. He knew it was just a fantasy, however.

"Our custody just sort of happened three years ago. When Alan was eleven, he came to us for the summer, he stayed for the year, and he's been with us ever since.

"During the three years before he came to live with us, he developed a fairly strong relationship with his stepfather, a man who at times was quite cruel to Alan, who had a history of having been in jail and having been an addict himself before starting a halfway house for other addicts. Today he's straightened himself out, but still he's not the best model for Alan, with his motorcycles, black leather jackets, and style of violence. Yet Alan still feels an attachment to this man as a person and as a model of manhood. No wonder, then, that Alan himself got into a period of violence and destruction.

"Rachel felt that I had arbitrarily agreed to take custody without discussing it with her. Before we were married she never really considered what could happen: that Alan could come to live with us permanently.

"I too certainly had mixed feelings about it. He created a

tremendous amount of tension in the family and a great deal of resentment on Rachel's part, despite the fact that she cared deeply for Alan.

"Rachel felt that in some way Alan was undermining my relationship with our child, Gary. She would point out that I spent far more time with Alan than with Gary, paid far more attention to my son than to our son. Sure I did—but an eleven-year-old is infinitely more interesting than a toddler. That's normal even in a nonstep relationship.

"I really think that today Rachel sees Alan as her own child. As for Alan, he's still somewhat torn, but he's aware of his mother's shortcomings and seems able to love her all the same and to love Rachel as well.

"Time and more time resolves things. There was a growing love on Rachel's part. There were times when I felt torn between my child and my wife, but you work things out. Certainly I was guilty of overindulging Alan, at a cost to us.

"We got through the bad year or so by being totally open with each other. We tried to face the problems together, not often in front of the children but with each other. We managed to keep on top of them.

"A great deal of the time we handled things by getting away by ourselves. There was a time when we were spending a night or two a week in New York. We were shoring up our sense of togetherness.

"Another thing we did that helped enormously was getting Alan into capable psychiatric hands. The sessions obviously speeded his improvement—it was a pleasure to watch. Alan's treatment started in December and ended in June. The psychiatrist saw Rachel and me four times. She didn't particularly approve of our going to New York so much. She said that parents should be on hand for the child. Well, we felt that parents should be on hand for the parents.

"One thing I wanted tremendously to put a stop to was the resentment that Alan had toward Rachel. He would show it by trying to undermine her with me. He would come to me and say he didn't think Rachel was being fair about this or that, often something to do with Gary. He was constantly coming up with some characteristic of Rachel's that he was unhappy about. I don't think he was doing it out of malice, or even consciously.

"At such times, I would call Rachel in and the three of us would all discuss the issue, whatever it was. There were two other ways in which we tried to stop it. Together we would include Alan more, direct more of our conversation to him. And we would be physically affectionate toward him, sometimes both—at the same time—putting our arms around him and hugging him. We tried to make him feel loved.

"We had agreed on some basics: that Alan be given a great deal of love, that he be encouraged to express his feelings—good or bad—and that he not be put under physical punishment.

"In hindsight, we were a little too indulgent with him. We both should have been firmer. By not being stronger, we made him feel more like a guest than a child in the home.

"Yet it's amazing that in three years we have become so strong. At this point it seems so far from stepchild-in-the-family.

"I had to recognize that all the resentment of Alan wasn't coming from Rachel—a lot of it was coming from me. He was terribly interruptive, and at times he seemed a genius at creating tension. But you overcome it. You talk, you share your feelings with your wife. You've got to. Or you go out and drink heavily, take up with another woman—avoid the situation."

LEGAI AND FINANCIAL TANGLES

Sometimes during a fight, Nancy would think about leaving Bruce. But how would she live? Of course, Nancy was for women's liberation, had always been for women earning equal amounts for equal jobs, and being given equal opportunity to get those jobs. And yet she had chosen to live her life traditionally, and now they were changing the rules midway in her life. She figured that women had turned the gun on men, and they had turned it right back on the women. Now here she was, caught. She had designed her life by the wrong set of ground rules.

Before they were married, she'd gotten alimony and child support. Now she only got a small amount of child support, and the chances of ever getting more from Carl were minuscule, she felt. She didn't own anything; even the house was in Bruce's name. She doubted she could get much money from Bruce for very long, as they had no children together. And what kind of a job could she get at this point in her life? Surely not enough to live with her family in dignity.

Many women find themselves in similar positions. We have found mothers and stepmothers who simply have not recognized the fact that, should this current family not go on forever, they will not receive the same kind of compensation that was available to them in the first marriage, unless of course they have children with this husband. The law as it now stands does not recognize a stepmother's rights to compensation for her services. The courts tend not to award alimony for any period of time, but rather temporary maintenance which permits a woman a couple of years to go out and find a job (despite the fact that she may never have worked as anything but a housewife before).

One attorney we interviewed proclaimed that women today have gotten themselves the equal right to get financially dealt out in a divorce. As far as money is concerned, women are getting less and less, he said.

Gail Linn, a Denver lawyer, told us that he recommends that a mother about to remarry, in order to protect herself under the existing law, persuade her new husband to adopt her children if at all possible. He cites the fact that she usually gives up financial support for herself from the prior husband when she remarries. Should the new marriage fail, her husband obviously will not be responsible for the support of her children.

On the other hand, to stepfathers he says his recommendation would have to be never to adopt because then he would be financially and legally responsible for the stepchild.

Mr. Linn goes on to discuss the deplorable lack of laws protecting steppeople. He cites the Colorado case of a woman who had been married to a widower for eleven years. At the time of the marriage the children were one and two years old. This woman never thought of adopting these children: she considered them her own. They remembered no other mother. After eleven years of marriage, her husband wanted a dissolution of marriage (divorce), which he obtained. She received half of the equity in the house and $200 a month for two years. The saddest part was that she was given no visitation rights to see her stepchildren. Tragically, the stepmother and stepchildren had no legal rights to see each other despite their close relationship. The case was appealed and appealed, but the decision held.

Nancy could have accepted Bruce's children all summer, every summer. If Bruce had accepted her children. If his children weren't so cruel to Kim. If she'd felt she'd had any say in their coming.

She didn't. It was something Bruce and his ex had decided together. Just when she'd looked forward to being alone with Bruce without the interference of children—hers were going to camp—*his* were coming for the whole summer.

The inequality of it all! Bruce, the man who objected to either of them doing the barest minimum for her children, would do anything for his.

WHEN HIS CHILDREN CAME

Everything changed when his children came.

The adult cocktail hour just went out the window. All year she'd been telling her Kim and Bobby that this was her and Bruce's sacred time alone together. Then along came Margie and Tory, and Bruce invited them in. Even an idiot could read the message: Bruce's children were more welcome than hers.

Suddenly everything was permitted or excused. At least for Margie and Tory. They weren't expected to do their share of the work. Bedtime was a moveable feast. But during the rest of the year, just let Bobby or Kim not do their chores or go to bed a few minutes late!

Having Tory and Margie meant so much to Bruce, of course, and it did at least give them the chance to act like a family. But damnit, Kim was sensitive and Margie could be just plain vicious. She'd walk all over Kim, hurting her in little ways whenever she got a chance. She'd look at Kim, who'd been crying, and say,

"What happened to your complexion? You look awful!" She'd have her friends over and not make a single gesture to include Kim. The same with Tory. She'd taunt and tease endlessly. And take things.

Once Nancy had told Bruce, Tory, Margie, anybody else who would listen, that she wasn't going to take care of other people's children if they went after her children. "Why should I do for them, when they do against mine?" There was an inexorable logic to her position, but Bruce didn't seem to grasp it.

The competition between the girls. She hated it. Who was the prettiest, the smartest, the most popular, the best dancer, the best athlete?

STEPSIBLING HOSTILITIES

For many parents the most rewarding part of living in step is the friendships between the children. These relationships can bring the whole family closer together. Children have told us that stepsiblings brought them closer to their own blood siblings, or that their stepbrothers and sisters become their closest friends. In such an instance the parent with custody is enormously rewarded.

For other parents, the sibling relationships are the most frustrating and wounding part of the merger, especially at the beginning of the marriage.

As every parent knows, siblings can act as a powerful guiding and teaching force in a younger child's life—often more so than his parents. They can also act as a destructive force. The older child is in a great position of power. A six-year-old, for example, may seem very powerful indeed to a two-year-old. If behind that power there is the angry force of stepsibling rivalry, the young child may be in an extremely vulnerable position. Steady parental intervention, quieting the angry child, inducing him to direct his hostility elsewhere, is strongly suggested.

We have seen parents fail to defend their children against the onslaughts of the stepsiblings—out of fear for the marriage, or the desire to win or keep the friendship of the stepchildren. In step we get caught up doing, or failing to do, things that we would or wouldn't otherwise do. Most mothers wouldn't hesitate to stop one of their children from being cruel to the other. She knows she is helping them both by stopping the behavior. The stepparent often bends over backward in trying not to favor his or her own child. In so doing, the parent virtually sets up the child as the victim of hostile assaults, verbal or nonverbal.

Nancy could stop Margie and Tory from being cruel to Kim. Instead, she lets it go on—and resents her stepchildren bitterly.

Part of the problem lies in expecting too much from stepchildren. Parents often expect stepsiblings to behave just like ideal blood siblings. Yet the children themselves don't expect these stepchildren to behave in some strange, nurturing, and wonderful way. Kids just being kids can seem extraordinarily cruel to the parent while to the child it just seems like tough normal kid behavior.

Parents can encourage and allow for supportive behavior between stepsiblings. Whenever they spot a supportive act—no matter how small—they can notice and reward it. "Freddy, thanks for taking the time to throw the ball with Johnny. You've helped him a lot—you're a good teacher."

Reward one act and you may get still another, and another, and another. Eventually, who knows, you might even get a basically good relationship.

It works, not only with one's children, but with one's mate as well. Positive reinforcement is vital in step and is one of the biological parent's best allies.

Okay, we hear you saying, there's not much to be thankful for! Stop complaining and ask for something. Too often we build up our grievances into one interminable lament, when all we had to do was to make a few firm requests.

Start with something small at first. Ask for it. When you get it, tell your partner how happy it's made you. Show how much it's meant to your child—perhaps it's something that only that stepparent could have done for that child. Say so. Arrange for events and express your gratitude for the good parts that happen. The evolution is slow, but as you go on the idea of reinforcement will soon come naturally to you. After a while, it's just possible that reinforcement will no longer be necessary. The stepchildren and stepparent will reward each other.

THE BOY WHO WALKED LIKE HIS STEPFATHER

She'd first noticed it one afternoon when she was sitting in the car waiting for Bruce and Bobby. Nearsighted as she was, she could still spot Bruce at a distance by his walk. Now she was noticing the identical walk of a somewhat smaller person. Bobby. Fourteen years old now. Gesture for gesture, step for step, the same as his stepfather. She laughed. When they got to the car, she said, "Hey, did you guys know you walk the same? No kidding, Bruce, Bobby walks just like you."

Another time she noticed it at dinner. There the two of them were, waiting for the soup to cool, two right hands resting lightly on the table in exactly the same position. After dinner, when Bobby had left the room, she mentioned it to Bruce.

"He's paying you a wonderful compliment. He's imitating you. He walks like you, copies your gestures, even wants to wear the same kind of clothes as you. Remember that old tie of yours you gave him? He wears it every chance he gets."

A pleased expression crossed Bruce's face. She noted it and decided to point out future similarities. Once she said, "You know, Bruce, he's copying your style. There's more of you in him than anyone."

There really was no doubt about it. Bobby had begun to identify with Bruce. He had taken an interest in whatever Bruce was interested in. Watching the hockey game on TV, fishing, playing poker.

She began to ask Bruce to do things with Bobby. Would he take him skiing, fishing, hunting? It would mean so much to Bobby.

Bruce was starting to give good messages to Bobby —from time to time—not just to Kim. Whenever Bruce did anything to encourage Bobby, she'd thank him. "Bruce, Bobby's not so secure—it's your approval he needs. Yours more than mine. Thanks for helping him."

If Bruce took Bobby fishing: "Thank you, Bruce. Just being around you shows him how a man can enjoy the outdoors. I can't do that. Only you."

It wasn't easy, but it was working. Three steps forward and two backward—well, at least the family was gaining ground.

At first she didn't know where she got the strength to be grateful for something so small as a smile or a pat on the back for her son. Or where she got the grace to keep her mouth shut when she wanted to scream. Or the courage to say straight out that thus and such was a major putdown of Bobby, and she wouldn't accept it. Or the power to speak out and ask for what she wanted.

But she did. She even quit bitching about his daughters' visits, figuring the family would never make it if she didn't. She tried to forgive, to understand what they all felt. The whole thing took so much maturity on her part, it was staggering.

She hoped that with time the good things would all happen without any effort on her part. She wanted to relax and just flow with it. Perhaps she could someday; perhaps she was fooling herself. She knew one thing: she wanted to keep that crazy guy Bruce and somehow manage to grow old with him. And she was willing to do whatever it took to make it work. Except, of course, to sacrifice her children.

Living in step was not, after all, being torn apart all the time. It was painful but challenging; tricky but rewarding; precarious but fun.

Like life itself: who ever said it would be a snap?

•/•

Bibliography

Baer, Jean. *The Second Wife: How to live happily with a man who has been married before.* Garden City, New York: Doubleday & Company, Inc, 1972.

Bergler, Edmund. *Divorce Won't Help.* New York: Hart, 1948.

Bernard, Jessie. "Remarriage of the Widowed and the Divorced," in Ruth S. Cavan, ed., *Marriage and the Family in the Modern World.* New York: Thomas Y. Crowell, 1960, pp. 416–424.

Bernard, Jessie. *Remarriage.* New York: The Dryden Press, 1956.

Bohannan, Paul. *Divorce and After.* Garden City, New York: Doubleday & Company, Inc, 1971.

Bowlby, John. *Attachment and Loss, Vol II, Separation, Anxiety and Anger.* New York: Basic Books, Inc, 1973.

Epstein, Joseph. *Divorced in America: Marriage in an Age of Possibility.* New York: E. P. Dutton & Co., 1974.

Fast, Irene and Albert C. Cain. "The Stepparent Role: Potential for Disturbances in Family Functioning," *American Journal of Orthopsychiatry,* XXVI (April 1966), pp. 485–491.

Fisher, Esther Oshiver. *Help for Today's Troubled Marriages.* New York: Award Books, 1968.

Furman, Erna. *A Child's Parent Dies: Studies in Childhood Bereavement.* New Haven and London: Yale University Press, 1974.

Gardner, Richard A. *The Boys and Girls Book About Divorce.* New York: Science House, 1970.

Goldstein, Joseph, Anna Freud, Albert J. Solnit. *Beyond the Best Interests of the Child.* New York: The Free Press, 1973.

Gordon, Thomas. *Parent Effectiveness Training.* New York: Peter H. Wyden, Inc, 1970.

Grimm, The Brothers. *Grimms' Fairy Tales.* New York: Grosset & Dunlap, 1965.

Hunt, Morton M. *The World of the Formerly Married.* New York: McGraw-Hill Book Company, 1966.

Laing, R.D. *The Politics of the Family and other essays.* New York: Random House, 1969.

Lowe, Patricia Tracy. *The Cruel Stepmother.* Englewood Cliffs, New Jersey: Prentice-Hall, Inc., 1970.

Satir, Virginia. *Conjoint Family Therapy.* Palo Alto, California: Science and Behavior Books, Inc., 1967 revised ed.

———. *Peoplemaking.* Palo Alto, California: Science and Behavior Books, Inc, 1972.

Schulman, Gerda L. "Myths that intrude on the adaptation of the stepfamily," *Social Casework,* (March 1972) pp. 131–139.

Simon, Anne W. *Stepchild in the Family.* New York: The Odyssey Press, 1964.

Steinzor, Bernard. *When Parents Divorce: A New Approach to New Relationships.* Pantheon Books, 1969.